GET BACK TO WORK

Smart & Savvy Real-World Strategies to Make Your Next Career Move

Melissa Washington

FriesenPress

Suite 300 – 852 Fort Street
Victoria, BC, Canada V8W 1H8
www.friesenpress.com

ISBN
978-1-4602-4443-2 (Hardcover)
978-1-4602-4444-9(Paperback)
978-1-4602-4445-6 (eBook)

Distributed to the trade by The Ingram Book Company

Table of Contents

To my Grandma,
You said I can do anything I put my mind to. Miss you!

To my Husband and Daughter,
Love you both so much!

To my Parents,
Thank you!

Introduction

Get Back to Work is for those seeking to make their next career move, from military members transitioning out of service to military spouses, from students graduating from college to mothers and fathers transitioning back into the workforce, from the unemployed to the underemployed, and from entrepreneurs in transition to those looking for their next opportunity.

In other words, this book is written for you.

I wrote *Get Back to Work* to offer people of all walks of life and at all career levels looking for work, smart and savvy real-world strategies and specific tools that can be applied directly to each individual situation. This book is like having a career guidance counselor, networking specialist, and best friend right at your fingertips. Although the task of finding work is ultimately up to you, I can guarantee that after reading this book you will be ahead of your competition, more agile in your career-seeking journey, and better prepared to tackle whatever job-seeking challenges come your way.

There's an added dimension to why I wrote this book. As a career woman with years of experience in recruiting and staffing, I also learned firsthand what it is like to lose a job. This experience, however, also reinforced my belief that when one door closes, another opens. By sharing my personal journey of unemployment and adventures in looking for work, I hope to inspire, motivate and encourage you as you navigate your own path.

In late 2009, I was laid off from what I believed was a secure job in the staffing industry due to a failing economy. This marked the beginning of a nearly two-year journey and career reinvention. Looking back I now realize how bittersweet that moment of being "let go" was for me.

Having worked in different recruiting roles for more than 10 years, I thought I would surely find another job quickly. As it turned out, however, the days turned into months and the months turned into years—almost two years, to be exact.

During this time of career transition and reinvention, I discovered many valuable tools to use when looking for work, the most helpful of which I will share with you in this book. Other sources might list tools that could come in handy during a job search; my goal is to ensure that you know exactly how to use them. My firm belief is that a tool is wasted if you don't learn how to use it properly.

Reflecting back on my years of looking for work, it's astonishing to see how much things have changed. It wasn't that long ago, in the time before e-mail and the Internet, that finding a job simply meant checking newspaper ads and using a fax machine to submit a résumé. Next was the explosion of the World Wide Web, which featured job boards and increased opportunities to find potential employers online.

And now here we are, in the digital era, with social media dominating the online world, and revolutionizing the hiring process for both employers and those seeking work. The need for resources, like this book, features up-to-date strategies and tools for how to best make your next career move.

Although *Get Back to Work* is organized by chapters, please feel free to skip around, because what is most important to you is what matters. Everyone's job-seeking needs and priorities are different, my goal is to provide guidance on a range of issues, from self-care while job seeking to proper conduct once you score that coveted interview. *Get Back to Work* is designed with *you* in mind, including a helpful space at the end of each chapter to write down notes and goals to help you stay on track. The back of the book has several BONUS tool's for your immediate use: LinkedIn Checklist, Looking for Work Checklist, Job and Networking Resource list, Veteran Resource list, and a master application.

Finally, note that I won't bore you with statistics about the job market or the economy (are you sighing with relief?). When in career transition, you're likely well aware of this information and tired of hearing it! So instead, we'll get right to the point and focus on the most pertinent tips and tools. *Get Back to Work* is all about guiding you to best utilize today's smart and savvy real-world strategies for making your next career move. And hopefully, it will help you land a career opportunity that you will truly enjoy, just as I have.

So what are you waiting for? Read on, and let's get you back to work!

Ten Things to Remember When You Are Looking for Work

1. File for unemployment benefits immediately after your job ends, even if you do not think you will qualify. Different states vary in whom they consider eligible.

2. Don't answer the phone if you don't recognize the number, as it could be someone calling you about a job. Instead, let the person leave a message so you can take time to prepare.

3. When you are looking for work, remember that you are now in sales and marketing. You need to brand and market your skills and abilities, and *you* have to be the one to make it happen. You can do it!

4. Don't let concerns about your age get in the way of applying for jobs you know you are qualified to do and physically perform.

5. Write down three goals for yourself on a piece of paper and post it in a place where you will see it every day. Make sure one of the goals is how much money you would like to make.

6. Carry a flash drive with your résumé, cover letter, and references. You never know when you might need them!

7. Before applying for any position, always look up the company on LinkedIn to see who you know that works there. Contact that person to obtain more information about the company. They may also be able to submit your résumé on your behalf.

8. Stay current. Read trade publications, comment on industry blogs, and be aware of emerging technologies that may impact your career path.

9. Technology has changed the way we look for work. Use smartphone apps. Many of the websites that I have listed at the back of this book also have apps.

10. Create a good, short response to the question - *Why should I hire you?*

Choose a job you love, and you will never have to work a day in your life.

—Confucius

1

First Steps

No matter why you are looking for work, it is very important for you to take care of yourself. Whether you were laid off, a college grad, are transitioning out of the military, have recently relocated, or are just ready for something new, looking for work can be stressful.

Stay Active

The first thing to remember when you start looking for work is to not to get stuck on the couch. You have to get up and move. Although joining a gym might not be in your budget right now, you can still take a walk around the block to get some fresh air, clear your mind, and prepare yourself for the task ahead. Nicki Crapotta, a fitness expert and personal trainer, shares:

> There are many options in your home for a rejuvenating workout. Body-weight exercises like push-ups, squats, and crunches can be done anywhere in the house with limited space. Some of the most effective and challenging exercises can be done on a mat and/or with a pair of dumbbells. Furthermore, thousands of training resources for the home, outdoors, and fitness center are at your fingertips via the Internet and smartphone apps.

Keeping fit will help you maintain your self-esteem, health, and overall well-being. This in turn, will make you feel better overall and lead to successful interviews. If you were involved with a hobby or sport while employed, try to stick to it during your transition.

Create a Workspace and Daily Schedule

The next thing to remember when you begin looking for work is that from this point forward—*looking for work is your full-time job* until you land your next position. Keeping this in mind, you will need to do the following:

- Create a workspace at home (if possible).

- Create a schedule of realistic goals you want to accomplish for the day (use the worksheet in Appendix B).

- Set a reward for yourself for meeting these goals.

- Track these goals on a spreadsheet or in a notebook, along with important meetings, connection with target companies, résumé submittals, phone screens, and interviews (in person and phone).

One way I was able to keep sane during my period of looking for work was by creating a work schedule and sticking to it. This required a change in my mindset, as I had to recognize that I was "working"—I was just not getting paid. I would begin my daily routine by dropping my daughter off at school in the morning. My parents (thank goodness for them!) would get her when school was over for the day, and then I would pick her up at their house by 5:30 p.m. Having this schedule allowed me to search for work during the day.

Here is an example of a daily schedule:

7:00 a.m. – Get up, dress up, eat breakfast, and exercise
8:30 a.m. – Check e-mails for job alerts and social media engagements
9:30 a.m. – Attend job-networking group
12:00 p.m. – Grab lunch with friend to practice for interview
2:00 p.m. – Attend informational interview with Target Company #1
3:30 p.m. – Send out thank-you card to informational interview contact,

check e-mails for job alerts, follow up with target list of companies

4:30 p.m. – Research companies and jobs

As you can see from the above example, less time should be spent on job boards and more time on getting out of the house. Manage your time wisely.

Find a Way to De-Stress when Needed

When I began looking for work, I quickly recognized that transitioning from one career to another can be a frustrating and discouraging process. Sometimes my e-mails went unanswered, the employers I contacted were not responsive, or informational interviews did not turn into a substantial lead. There was also the stress caused by family members, who questioned why I could not find work.

To deal with these stressors, I decided to use some of my time to work on at-home projects I had on my to-do list—projects such as making a scrapbook for my daughter, cleaning out the junk drawer, doing some much-needed gardening, and organizing the Tupperware cabinet. It lifted my spirits to mark these items off my list, I received a positive reward for finishing a task, and there was no cost involved. For men, de-stressing projects can include cleaning out those cabinets in the garage or finally painting the man cave.

Diana Conwell, a licensed marriage and family therapist, career counselor, and life coach, has some great advice on taking "time off" from looking for work:

> Although it is hard to put anxieties aside about finances and responsibilities, you can't live and breathe your job search 24/7. You have permission to have time off! Likewise, you have permission to have a life beyond your job search.

> When I said this to a group of job seekers once, a man in the group said, "I wish I would have heard that before now!" He explained that he had not seen his family for more than four years, and he had just visited them in another state over the holiday. He said, "I sat there all during Thanksgiving dinner thinking, *I should be looking up jobs to apply for right now. I wonder if I got a response to the last application I sent out. Did Bill e-mail me back about the LinkedIn connection?*"

The man said he had been so worried about keeping a constant vigil over his job search that he really could not enjoy his family or his time off. His job search was completely wearing him down, because there was no balance with the other necessary parts of his life.

Giving yourself permission to take time off from looking for work will help you deal with the frustrating and depressing parts of the process. But of course, if you find that you are depressed often, don't neglect this; seek treatment from an experienced professional.

Create a "Thankful" List

Another great way to help you feel good about yourself is to make a list of all the things for which you are thankful. Reminding yourself frequently of all the blessings you have in your life will help you put your career transition into proper perspective.

Focus

Each day, focus on where you want to be. This can be done by meditating, praying, or just taking a few minutes out for yourself. Don't just think about it, dream it! And write it down. I have a "dream board" this is where I post photos of my dream vacation spots, my dream house, my dream car, my dream private jet (equipped with a pilot, of course!), and so on. Then I have my white board of immediate objectives that I want to attain or accomplish, this can be a certain type of job, salary, company, et cetera.

A goal is a dream with a deadline. —Napoleon Hill

Take Care of Your Finances

Finally, when you are not bringing in the amount of income that you were when working, it is important to properly manage your finances. Perhaps you received a severance package or have a savings account that you can tap into while looking for work.

Cover your bases when cutting down on costs. Look for ways to lower your monthly bills including:

- cable

- car insurance

- electric

- phone

- water and trash service providers

Ask what programs the companies who provide these services have to offer. Some companies have hardship plans or level-payment plans for which you might qualify. Discontinue cable channels you don't watch and get rid of any extra phone lines or services you are not using. Sometimes when companies learn that you want to cancel your services, they will try to keep your business by offering you a discount.

If you own a house, look for ways to lower your monthly mortgage payment. When I was looking for work, we tried to refinance our mortgage, but we hit a roadblock when the bank told us we had too much debt. This was frustrating, as the reason we needed the help was that I had lost my income. Today, there are better programs out there to help homeowners, so make sure to explore the possibilities.

If you are struggling to pay the bills, work with your creditor. If you are unable to work out a payment plan, consider contacting a reputable non-profit credit counseling organization.

Collect some extra income by selling off items you no longer need. Have a garage sale, or sell stuff on Craigslist and eBay. During my "downtime," I went through my house, purged, and made some cash. Turn a hobby into an income stream: pet sitting, offering music lessons, art lessons, coaching, or refereeing all provide potential income opportunities while looking for work.

Shop at discount, thrift, and consignment stores. It's amazing what kinds of quality clothes can be found at these places. Sometimes you may have to dig to find a bargain, but they are there. Most of my daughter's quality clothing comes from these stores, especially since she is in a new size each year. I can no longer justify spending $20 for a pair of pants that she is only going to wear for a short period of time.

Clip coupons, you can find them in the newspaper and online. When I shop at any store or go to a restaurant, I use two apps on my smartphone—RetailMeNot and Entertainment Book—to see if I can find any discounts. I also ask if the establishment offers an AAA or a military discount. Another company that gives discounts, if you qualify for them, is AARP. Just be prepared to show your ID.

To Do and/or Goals:

_____

_____

_____

_____

_____

2

Support Resources

If you are laid off and your company offers an outplacement service, take advantage of it. In addition, there are a lot of resources in your local area that may offer services such as Internet access, listings of current job openings, career information, résumé and interview preparation, community referrals, vocational training opportunities, and career workshops. Seek out organizations in your community that help people looking for work, such as the Employment Development Department (EDD), One-Stop Career Center, AARP, YMCA, and the Latter Day Saints Employment Resource Services.

A great resource for women is www.WhatsforWork.com. This is a valuable community for women who are entering the job market for the first time to those who are returning, and those who want to make a change.

Also consider visiting public libraries, houses of worship, your local chamber, college career centers, veteran's services, or job clubs, and enlisting the help of career and life coaches. Use at least two of these resources as you are searching for work, you will find them to be beneficial. Appendix C lists some additional resources.

Job Clubs

There is nothing wrong with you if you attend a job club. Everyone in the club had a job at one time or another and they all found themselves in this situation due to different circumstances. In fact, individuals looking for work can be a valuable resource to you.

I was once one of those job club members. It was the beginning of 2010 and I had applied for many different positions. I had been in recruiting for more than 10 years, and I thought I was doing everything right. One day, I saw in the local paper that a professional networking group was meeting at the local EDD. I had been in my area for less than two years and knew that I needed to start networking and make some connections. So I signed up. The group met once a week, brought in some great local speakers, and had informative workshops.

During this time, I started to reconnect with acquaintances on LinkedIn, which I had joined back in 2004 (member number 1,408,083). At one point, people in my job-networking group started to ask me how to use LinkedIn. I began helping people on an individual basis and then started conducting workshops at my dining room table. Typically, I would meet with five to seven people for about two hours and show them how to build a profile and use it to find work. The workshops were designed to be hands-on, so I would project my profile on the wall and ask people to follow along on their laptops. I did not charge to conduct these workshops because I was receiving unemployment benefits at the time.

Many success stories came from those trainings. One of them was John Quinn, whom I met in early 2010 at a job-seeking group. He came and sat at my dining room table in May of that year, not sure about how using LinkedIn could help him, but he was open to giving it a try. John took what I taught, built his profile and connected with people with whom he had worked with over 10 years ago. Like many people, John did not initially see the benefit of connecting with someone he had worked with so long ago and who lived in another state. But soon enough, the advantages became apparent to him. Here is what John had to say after securing a new job through contacts reestablished on LinkedIn:

> I found and linked in with people I had worked with over my 12-year career with Standard Register. One of the individuals I reconnected with was Rod Stone, whom I had worked for as Marketing Manager of the Label Division at Standard Register. From the first day Rod and I got linked in and exchanged phone numbers, to the day I got my new job offer with Prime Labeling Systems within weeks, this never would

have happened without Melissa's LinkedIn training and mentoring. I have used this LinkedIn training to reconnect with so many people I had lost contact with. I am continuing using LinkedIn to try to get new contacts for my new position as Sales Director with Prime Labeling Systems.

John learned the importance of reconnecting with people, as you never know what opportunities or assistance they might be able to provide. Had John not reconnected with Rod, Rod would not have known that John was living and looking for work in a different state.

Active Job Seekers of America

Active Job Seekers of America (AJSA) provides support, networking, and employment opportunities to individuals both online and offline. This group and others like it—for example, Neighbors Helping Neighbors on the East Coast or SING in the San Francisco Bay Area are great places for people looking for work to encourage one another when seeking employment, a priceless perk of joining the organization.

I became aware of AJSA after completing a job-networking course and meeting with Steven Lease, who founded the group in Auburn, California in 2009 after being laid off from his job at Intel Corporation. Steven started the group out of a desire to meet with other individuals who were also going through the job-seeking process. Over time, many people heard about the group and joined.

When I met Steven, he was in the process of starting another job club in Roseville, California. I became President of that group, and our membership grew from just two to a consistent 40 per week. I felt it was important to share this leadership opportunity with others who were looking for work so that they could practice their leadership skills. To make this happen, Steven and I created an Executive Director position where I was responsible for club activities at the Auburn, Folsom, and Roseville locations. Today, I continue to volunteer in this position to help people in transition.

Several members of the Roseville group put a charter together. Those in the group had always believed that with all the talent in the room, we could form our own company. We used our collective talent to create our own website, www.

ActiveJobSeekers.org. We established a presence on LinkedIn with a company page—Active Job Seekers of America—and a LinkedIn group page with sub-groups for local chapters. Today, we can also be found on Facebook (facebook. com/ActiveJobSeekersofAmerica) and Twitter (@ActiveJobSeeker). Please "like" and follow us!

AJSA is set up so anyone can start a club. The groups begin with introductions and announcements—someone shares his or her experience about getting a job or offers job leads, job resources, job fairs, and ways to promote the group. Following the introduction, there is a discussion session on relevant topics or an outside speaker is brought in. The meeting concludes with each person creating three goals—at least one of which he or she can control. This format helps attendees polish their public speaking skills-there is no way to hide in the corner and not participate. One of the best things about AJSA is that members who find a job are encouraged to come back and share their success stories.

I remember once being approached by a woman who was a first-timer to our group. As we chatted after the meeting, she confessed that she had been hesitant to come, as she had been told that job groups did not help people and that everyone who attended were depressed, which would in turn would make her depressed. Her experience was quite the opposite; she told me that she was so glad that she had. She found the group meeting to be refreshing and resourceful giving her the tools that she could put to use. She came back each week until she eventually found a job.

I recommend you attend different job clubs like AJSA in your area. Find the one that is right for you.

An Accountability Partner/Mentor

When you are looking for work, it is important to find an accountability partner. Such a person will not only keep you accountable but also will help keep you motivated. An accountability partner can be a life coach or someone who is also in career transition. Hold yourself accountable by sharing your plans your accountability partner-sharing your plans and goals out loud to someone else, and having them follow up with you, often results in increased productivity.

In addition to an accountability partner, you may want to form your own "board of directors" or "advisory board." These should be people you trust to give you encouragement and honest feedback about your strengths and weaknesses.

Good people for this type of role include mentors, friends, and previous colleagues or bosses.

Be sure to seek out individuals who will give you support, not advice (there is a big difference between the two.) You also want people who will support you in doing what is right for *you*, not them. You should surround yourself with those who will help you make decisions that are consistent with your goals and strengths.

I have found that there are so many people who want to help with mentoring. Places to look would be local chambers and other organizations, or just type in "mentor" on Google with your local city to see what comes up.

As Diana Conwell, the counselor and life coach introduced earlier, notes:

> The first part of your job search may include attending to what I call "head and heart issues" such as anger, anxiety, grief, fear, loss of self-esteem, depression, confusion, or hopelessness that result from job or career loss. We are often aware that one of these emotions is there—especially if we have lost a job or career—but we don't always do something about it. Oftentimes, several of these emotions or mental health issues are present. Getting support from someone who can help you sort it all out is thus an essential first step in the job-search process. If you are feeling stuck in your job search, this might be the place to look to avoid sabotaging your best efforts.

Many people I speak with after they have been rejected for a job want to give up. Don't give up, instead persevere. We all have setbacks in life. Refocus your goals and reconnect with your accountability partner to get back on track and keep the momentum going.

To Do and/or Goals:

_____

_____

_____

_____

_____

3

Your Brand

You have probably heard people talk about "creating a personal brand." As you look for your next career opportunity, identifying a strong personal brand will give you a leg up on your competition. The concept of "personal branding" originated in an article featured in a 1997 issue of *Fast Company* magazine, by Tom Peters, a reputed American writer on business management practices. In his article, titled "The Brand Called You," Tom talks about running your career like a business—that is, becoming the CEO of your own business: Me, Inc. [1]

In 2010, I attended an event called Reinvent Your Future, hosted by CareerBuilder and University of Phoenix. The keynote speaker was Stedman Graham, New York Times best-selling author, educator, speaker and businessman. As I sat in the front row and listened to him speak, I was impressed not only because he was Oprah's boyfriend but more importantly by his journey and everything he had accomplished during his life. Through his company, S. Graham & Associates he trains individuals and organizations to maximize their potential by developing a strong identity.

Graham said one of the reasons Oprah has been so successful is that she has successfully done the same thing over and over: interview people. In other words, she created a strong *brand* and name for herself because she identified one thing she did especially well and worked at it. Graham asked everyone in the audience to consider an important question: "What do you want from life?" In order to answer this important question, you must first understand *who you are* and what influences your behavior. If you do not define yourself, outside forces will do it for you. [2]

Identify Your Skills and Interests

Where do you start in building a great personal brand? Oftentimes the things that you are good at doing are not really the things you *like* doing. You want to brand yourself around not only your skills but also your interests. I recommend that you begin by taking some time to write down answers to the following questions:

What are my main interests?

_____

What do I enjoy doing?

_____

What do other people come to me for?

_____

Who do I want to become?

_____

What makes me unique?

_____

What talents do I have that most people don't?

_____

How could this fit into today's marketplace?

_____

It may take you an hour or several days to answer these questions, but don't skip this important part of the branding process. As Judy Isaman, a career development mentor, states:

The workplace is changing, all the time. Organizations hire individuals whose brand mirrors the talent they need to move their strategies forward and meet and exceed goals. Your brand is a reflection of you, and it communicates how you will be perceived and adapt to challenges. So, before targeting an organization, ask yourself, *What does my brand message convey to others? What value will I bring to a potential employer?*

Determine Your Strengths

Identifying your skills, talents, and abilities will help you differentiate yourself from the competition. There are many personality assessments and books that can help you do this. One excellent resource is *Now, Discover Your Strengths* by Marcus Buckingham, which comes with access to an online assessment tool. Another great book by Buckingham is geared towards women: *Find Your Strongest Life: What the Happiest and Most Successful Women Do Differently*. Some online resources are included in Appendix C.

One book that you are probably familiar with is *What Color is your Parachute* by Richard N Bolles. The first edition was released back in 1972 and every year Mr. Bolles updates this classic with relevant and up-to-date information. While lengthy, I would recommend reading it if you have time. One of its best takeaways is the Self-Inventory (The Flower Exercise), which provides a good inventory of your likes and dislikes, and may help with figuring out what path to take. I had the pleasure of being the opening speaker and introducing Mr. Bolles in 2011 at a career event in the Bay Area.

Once you identify your strengths, you can begin to formulate strategies on how to identify the opportunities you want. From there, you can create what is referred to as a personal introduction, or "elevator pitch." The term elevator pitch comes from this hypothetical scenario: if you were in an elevator for a brief moment with the CEO of a company that you were interested in, and you had only 30 seconds or less to make a pitch, what would you say? Just remember that you have unique talents and abilities that you may not yet have tapped into. Creating your brand identity is free—it just takes time to figure it out.

Train Your Mind to Be Positive

It is easy for people who are in career transition to fall into the trap of feeling ashamed or embarrassed because they are not working. In our country, people often tie their identities to a job title and where they work; it is almost as if they have handed their career identities over to their employers. Most of this stems from baby boomers, as they tend to view their careers and themselves as one and the same. But times have changed. We now recognize that we are much more than our job titles.

Every year local business journals acknowledge 40 people under 40 that are making their mark in leadership, community involvement and entrepreneurship. In 2011, while I was still unemployed, I was chosen as one of the winners of the *Sacramento Business Journal* "40 under 40" prestigious award. This came as quite a surprise, as I didn't think the organization would give an award like that to someone who was not working. In fact, I was the only winner who was unemployed, which shows that you don't have to have a paid job to provide value or be recognized. I received the award for my leadership with AJSA and for helping people get back to work.

My experience shows that it is worth spending time thinking about who you are and your personal brand. Train your mind to be positive and turn off the doubts about your situation. Turn "unemployed" into "searching for new opportunities." *You are not less of a person because you do not have a job.*

Perhaps Suzy Welch, a best-selling author and noted business journalist, put it best at a Chick-fil-A Leadercast event that I attended: "What do you want people to say when you are not in the room?" This is a great question to ask yourself. Have the courage to be who you are! Now might be the time to reinvent yourself, as there will never be that "perfect" time to do it.

Learn Something New

After figuring out what you want to do, you may want to go back to school. There are a lot of schools that offer classes in the evenings or other formats to accommodate for various schedule needs. If you have transitioned out of the military, make sure to look into the GI Bill. Can't afford tuition? Take a look at scholarships, grants, and loans.

A Pathway Without a Known Destination

Jim Carman, who leads the Transition Center at the Military Officers Association of America, offers some interesting insights about job transitions:

- For professionals who were long tenured in their last role, this may be the first time since college or graduate school when you find yourself on a pathway without a known destination. Accordingly, it's important to recognize that changing jobs is an intricate process that affects every member of your family. In addition to trying to find the right niche for your professional life, you must consider whether you are willing to relocate, disrupt your spouse's career and your children's schooling, and change your lifestyle to accommodate a potentially lower salary. And unlike military relocations and some corporate moves, in which stress is mitigated by sponsor programs and a supportive network on both ends of the move, this time you might be on your own.

- For senior military officers who have reached retirement eligibility, the most likely reasons to consider a career transition include a desire to support your spouse's career, develop geographic stability for your family, reaching statutory retirement or a missed promotion. Additionally, many senior officers would rather not end their careers as staff commandos – far removed from duty in operational units.

- Younger professionals, by contrast, have less invested emotionally and financially in their careers and are often more receptive to change. Their most frequent reasons for seeking different work include a desire of higher pay and greater responsibility, a preference for less family separation and more geographic stability, or a quest to find a more flexible career path.

- Regardless of the reasons that brought you to this crossroads, it's important to realize that military officers and other professionals have a wide variety of skills, experiences and passions to offer their next employer. And because you do many things well, you may find it difficult to assess what is right for you at this point in time. For example:

- Should I seek a position that utilizes my transferable military skills or embark on a radically new course?

- Should I go to a Fortune 500 company or seek a more free-wheeling entrepreneurial firm?

- Is now the time to buy a business, become a consultant, head to graduate school or enter public service?

- Would an international opportunity be a career-catapulting move at this time?

- Is this a time to seek outlets for aspects of your personality that haven't been previously expressed? Midlife is often a time when parts of the self that have been neglected begin to bubble up. Accordingly, this may be the time to do something that you have always wanted to do.

Finally, as you ponder these possibilities, ask yourself how much risk you are prepared to tolerate. Robert Rubin, Secretary of the Treasury in the Clinton Administration, always reminded his staff that "even the best decisions are probabilistic and run a real risk of failure."

To Do and/or Goals:

_____

_____

_____

_____

_____

4

Networking

You have probably heard it said: "It's not what you know; it's who you know." There is much truth to this statement. According to a report from ABC News, 80 percent of jobs are landed through networking.[3] Today, the contacts you make in the business world are some of the best ways for you to find new opportunities.

Your network can include previous co-workers, friends, neighbors, clients, members of professional organizations, professors, teachers, vendors, church members, people you served with in the military or other organizations, and school alumni. In the career transition process, your goal is to identify, build, and cultivate these relationships. But what if you don't know the first thing about networking? Well, there are some simple steps you can take to make networking—both offline and online—feel like much less of a chore.

Offline Networking – Get Up, Dress Up, and Show Up! [4]

I always tell people to "Get Up, Dress Up, and Show Up." If you sit on the couch or behind a computer all day, you are not going to make much happen. Once you do it, it can change your life.

To build your list of networking contacts, attend networking events hosted by associations, school alumni groups, chamber meeting groups, local groups, professional organizations, veterans' organizations, and others. A good site to check out to find these events is www.meetup.com. Also check your local paper, business journal, Facebook, and search Google.

Remember that a networking event does not have to be any of the more traditional types of events listed above. You can network at a church picnic, at a kid's soccer game, while standing in line at a movie theater, and so forth.

I attended many networking events when I was looking for work, and I still do today as a small business owner. There are so many different events held each day in which you can participate. Just try to find ones that are free to low cost, as it will be hard when you're unemployed to fork out money to attend an event.

Before you attend a networking event, first decide who you are going to connect with and make quality connections. For added motivation, if you bring someone with you, consider making the outing into a competition of who can acquire the most quality contacts. Secondly, prepare some open-ended icebreaker questions like:

1. How long have you lived in the area?

2. What type of work do you do?

3. What do you enjoy most about what you do?

4. How long have you been involved with this organization?

Also, check out the news before you go to the event so you can be up to date on current events in order to add to the conversation.

Have your "personal introduction" ready and be comfortable and prepared to share about yourself. You may think, "Who wants to speak to me since I don't have a job?" Remember that it's all about how you present yourself. Be confident and know what you are looking for. If you don't want to go alone to a networking event, bring someone from one of the job club groups that you attend. Work the room and *listen, listen, listen*. People love to share about their passions, and you may find someone with whom you share common interests. In addition, you may meet someone who has a problem you can solve, or you may be able to connect that person with someone who can offer a solution.

If there is a speaker at the event, check LinkedIn or Google to find out more about his or her background. This will ensure that you are prepared to speak to this person when he or she is done presenting. Most speakers make themselves after an event and want to speak with attendees. Be ready with what you want to accomplish when speaking with them.

If the networking event you are attending provides a badge for you to write your name on, make sure your writing is neat. Place your badge on the right side of your chest. That way, when someone shakes your hand, your name will be visible. Another idea is to have your own customized badge made that you can wear to events. I have my own magnetic badge (that way, the pin does not leave a hole in my clothing), which has my first and last names and my caricature.

If you make a good networking contact, be sure to get his or her card. Try to connect with that person on social media and LinkedIn, and follow up your conversation with an e-mail, a phone call, or even a handwritten note.

There are also apps out there to use, where you can simply scan the person's business card and save the information directly to your smartphone. What's great about these types of apps is that they date-stamp the information so you know exactly when you scanned it. It also keeps a photo of the card. Some of the apps will also connect you and the other person on LinkedIn.

I don't take business cards home anymore. If you were to hand me your business card, I would open up my app, take a picture of your card, and hand it right back to you. The app takes all the information off your business card and feeds it straight to LinkedIn where I can connect with you and save your information to my Outlook contacts. This system is truly convenient and efficient, and is quick and easy. There was an app that I used called CardMuch which has since been discontinued and LinkedIn has formed a partnership with Evernote which provides a similar function. I would recommend searching the app store for the business card reader that is right for you. This will also make you look tech-savvy, which in this day and age is a key skill. So go ahead and convert those business cards into contacts.

Try to attend a networking event at least once a month. Networking events provide value to members by bringing in speakers and having workshops, which may provide professional enhancement that will help you improve your knowledge and skills that may be applied when you get back to work. Remember to be yourself, and to be memorable.

It is especially essential to network when you move to a new area and do not know anyone. When I was a military spouse, networking was a key factor in finding work. If you are close to a military installation, find out what groups meet on base and off. This type of networking is a great way to find others with similar interests.

Your network can be a great resource to help you tap into the hidden job market (see chapter 6). You can even start your own networking group. In my case, I was a graduate of the University of Phoenix, so I reached out to the local campus to see if there was an alumni networking group. At the time such a group didn't exist, so I decided to start my own. I went onto LinkedIn, searched for alumni who lived in the Sacramento area, and connected with a few people. By 2010 we were having alumni dinners the last Wednesday of every month. After a few months, I reached out to the campus and gained the University's endorsement. Today it is officially part of the University of Phoenix Alumni Association and one of the larger active alumni groups.

Online Networking

Build your online network on social media platforms such as LinkedIn, Facebook, Twitter and Google+. And don't forget about e-mail. I am a firm believer that when building solid connections, it's not about the quantity as much as it is about quality. It's also important to update your status regularly on the social media platforms you use.

Let your network know that you are looking for a new opportunity, and be specific about the types of work you are seeking. When I was looking for work, I sent out a quarterly e-mail to my connections under the subject line, "Melissa Washington Update." In the first part of the e-mail, I let my contacts know specifically what types of opportunities I was hoping to pursue. In the second part, I added some bullet points about what I had been doing (such as volunteering). I then ended with a call to action, asking my contacts to please let me know about any opportunities. I also used this e-mail to ask my contacts to follow me on Twitter or connect with me on LinkedIn.

Career Fairs

Job fairs are still around, and they come in different forms. Be strategic before attending one and check out the list of employers that will be there. You may find that some job fairs still have multi-level marketing companies that will try to get you to join. Pursue these types of job fairs if that is something of interest to you; otherwise, focus your efforts on spending time with other employers. Make a list of employers that you want to meet and research them beforehand, just as you would prior to an interview. When doing the research also look at what their current openings are. Here are some ideas for where to conduct research online:

- Company website

- Glassdoor

- Google

- Hoovers

- LinkedIn

- Local business journal

- Local newspaper

- Manta

- Vault

Bring copies of your résumé (see chapter 12) and business cards (see chapter 5), and dress to impress. Leave your children and parents at home. Note that some employers do onsite interviews, so be ready and arrive early.

Be prepared for the possibility that an employer may not take your résumé and may instead instruct you to apply on its company website. Use this as a learning opportunity to find out more about the company. Also, use the occasion to find out from the employer what you should put on the application. Get these employers' business cards or contact information, and always remember to follow up. Use this opportunity to network with the other people there who are also looking for work.

Virtual Career Fairs

The first impression you make at a virtual career fair is going to be based on your online presence. So make sure to have your LinkedIn profile updated, as well as any other social media sites you use. Similar to what you would do prior to attending a face-to-face job fair, perform research beforehand on companies that will be in attendance.

Have your résumé uploaded in the virtual career fair environment. This type of career fair will take place, right from your computer. Even though you won't be face-to-face with potential employers and contacts, dress in your professional attire, comb your hair, and brush your teeth. It's okay to get out of your pajamas or sweats for a little bit. Take this seriously, as you want to look and feel the part of being in an interview.

Be ready with questions and answers. If you are not a fast typist, it's a good idea to have some questions and answers typed up in advance that you can simply copy and paste into the chat.

Finally, and no less importantly, remember to send a thank you e-mail and/or card to those with whom you had the opportunity to chat and network with.

To Do and/or Goals:

_____

_____

_____

_____

_____

5

Business/Networking Cards

Business cards (also referred to as networking cards) are not only for those employed by businesses. Anyone seeking a new opportunity should have a business card. They are a great networking tool, so have them ready and use them.

There are many different places where you can have business cards printed. Try www.vistaprint.com and www.gotprint.net on the Internet, or use a local print shop. You can also purchase business cards at an office supply store, Wal-Mart, or Target. Microsoft Word can even be used to create and print.

Your business card must include your name, phone number, professional e-mail address, customized LinkedIn URL, Twitter handle (if you tweet), and either a branding statement or the types of positions in which you are interested. If applicable, add any education, training, and/or certifications you have received as well. Make sure to design your card so that it is easy to read and has a nice look. Always use the front and back. Make it eye-catching and use a color photo or graphic; this will help people remember you.

For my business cards, I wanted something catchy that would build my personal brand. So what better way to do this than to have a caricature of myself on the card? I still use the same format today. When I started my training business, I began using tent cards, which I can easily stand up in front of attendees at my workshops.

While there is a growing trend with people wanting to be "green" and exchange information via smartphones instead of printing business cards, I would still recommend having cards on hand. You cannot assume that everyone keeps their contacts in digital form or online. You never want to miss an opportunity.

To Do and/or Goals:

_____

_____

_____

_____

_____

6

The Hidden Job Market

Many companies today do not post their jobs externally (on a job board or company website) because they already have a substantial database of candidates, a limited recruitment budget, and/or an excellent referral program. Or, quite simply, they may not want to be inundated with unqualified applicants. Additionally, some companies post jobs internally for a period of time before posting externally. CNN Money reports that 80 percent of available jobs go unadvertised.[5] This means that they get filled internally or through employee recommendations or from company applicant database. These unadvertised openings are what make up the "hidden job market." How can you tap into this hidden job market? Begin by making a list of at least five to seven companies where you would be interested in working and do research on them. There are a number of great online and offline resources including:

- Company website

- Glassdoor

- Google

- Hoovers

- LinkedIn

- Local business journal

- Local newspaper

- Manta

- Vault

Search local business publications, such as your local business journal, which offer free daily updates. This is a great resource to find out what companies are moving into the area or expanding it's current business.

Using LinkedIn, seek out anyone you know who works at the company you are interested in (a first-degree connection) or anyone who has a friend or an acquaintance (a second-degree connection). LinkedIn is a great platform to use to identify contacts you can leverage, as it allows you to do advanced searches by using specific keywords (additional information about how to use LinkedIn can be found in chapter 9). This is a great opportunity to tap into your college alumni!

The next step is to introduce yourself to representatives of the company or have one of your connections introduce you. Set up an informational interview or what I like to call an "informational meeting", as it creates less pressure. Try to meet company representatives at their office rather than a neutral meeting place like a coffee shop. Meeting them at their office provides you with the opportunity to check out the environment and people who work there. Also, the person you are meeting with may be able to introduce you to someone in the department that you are interested in working in. Remember the purpose of the informational meeting is to obtain information about the company, not to try to get a job. These types of meetings can also be beneficial if you are considering a new field of work.

Before attending such a meeting, ask yourself what you want to accomplish and make sure you have your personal introduction ready. Write down questions you want to ask, such as the following:

- Does the company have a career development plan?

- How long have you worked here?

- If you had a choice, would you make the same career decision again?

- May I connect with you on LinkedIn and keep in contact?

- What attracted you to the company and position?

- What challenges do you face?

- What do you need to do to be successful?

- What does a typical day look like for you?

- What is your role at this company?

Don't forget to thank the person for his or her time, follow up, and connect on LinkedIn if they are willing to do so. You want the person to remember you in the event an opportunity comes up in the future. Also, be sure to send the person a thank you card. By making such connections, you can gain an advantage over your competition.

Tony Restell, founder of Social-Hire.com, shares some great insight about why it's important to invest in your social media presence to maintain visibility to recruiters who are searching social media sites. Just as a side note, I'd also like to point out here *that social media can easily connect you to a global audience.* Consider my own experience as an example: through online networking, I connected with Tony, who lives in the United Kingdom. He has been a great resource for me as well as for people looking for work and recruiters. Here's what Restell has to say:

> In the last years there's been a huge change in the way companies recruit new talent—and you need to adapt! The most significant development is that the "hidden jobs market" has grown substantially. Did you know many of the world's leading companies have built teams of several thousands of internal recruiters—whose primary role is to try to fill positions without ever having to go through the usual advertising or recruitment agency routes?

But if you can't be considered for these openings by responding to job adverts or by working with recruitment agencies, how do you ensure you're not missing out? There are two key things to be aware of:

1. Companies making effective use of employee referral schemes powered by social networks are filling one-third of their openings via this route. These positions are forwarded on to people in the employee networks of a company, people who look like strong matches for the hiring profile at hand. But the process is mostly automated! Technology searches the social networks of all employees to find strong matches—and then prompts employees to forward vacancies on to their contacts, often with a financial inducement for doing so.

2. In addition to referral schemes, these new armies of internal recruiters are also scouring social networking sites, looking for potential fits for their company's openings beyond the reach of their current employees' networks. Potential matches are then approached directly about vacancies, often without those vacancies ever having been openly advertised.

There are two keys that help ensure you're in the running for lucrative openings in this "hidden jobs market." The first is ensuring that you have keyword-rich and fully complete profiles across all the major social networks. That's what maximises the chances of you appearing as a suitable candidate when a recruiter or an employee referral programme searches to find potential candidate matches. The best way I find to do this is to look at several job advertisements for the types of openings you aspire to secure. Skip to the "Must Have Experience" or "Desired Candidate Profile" section and make a note of all the things the recruiter wants successful candidates to be able to demonstrate. These are the exact things that a recruiter is likely to use as the basis for a search when looking for candidates. Then go to your social profiles and—as far as is truthful—make sure you've included all these keywords! Plus be sure to do this on all the major social platforms (LinkedIn, Google Plus, Facebook, and Twitter), since you never know where recruiters may be looking to fill that role you don't know about but would love to be offered!

Over and above getting your profiles right, it's also essential that you invest in building the size of your network as much as possible. Employee referral programmes scan the profiles of people who are in the networks of their existing employees. So it stands to reason that the more people whose networks you are in, the more times you will be considered by employee referral programmes as a potential fit for an opening. Similarly, given that recruiters are more inclined to hire someone who has some connection to the company already, the better networked you are, the more credible you will look as a candidate when they conduct their searches online.

Hopefully, you now understand why it's critical that you invest in your social media presence in ways that will get you onto the radars of recruiters—and the employee referral technologies that they have deployed. Recruiting has undergone a major evolution—and therefore, so too must your approach to your next job search!

To Do and/or Goals:

_____

_____

_____

_____

_____

7

The Contingent Workforce

As you continue to make your way through the job-hunting process, don't overlook the value of staffing companies. Staffing agencies are hired by companies to screen and hire candidates for either temporary, contract, temporary to permanent, and direct hire positions. Besides "temp agencies" or "staffing agencies," they may also be referred to as "headhunters," "executive search firms," "search firms," "retained search firms," or "contingency search firms."

Staffing agencies have a good pulse on the local job market and are typically the first to hire when the economy picks up. They can provide you with an opportunity to "check out" the company to which they assign you to see if it is a good place to work on a permanent basis. They also allow you to learn new skills and sharpen the ones you already have. In many cases, you never know where a temporary or contract job will lead.

A common misperception is that those who work for temporary agencies don't have the right education or skills to land a "permanent" job. In fact, when many people think of temps, they immediately picture someone in a receptionist-type position. Research by Randstad, the 2nd largest staffing company in the world, however, paints a different picture: the reality is that almost one-third of contingent workers are in managerial and supervisory roles. Furthermore, contractors and temps show more job satisfaction than permanent employees. [6] The new health care reform is also giving contingent workers benefits that they never had previously.

The Rise of Supertemps

The *Harvard Business Review* defines "supertemps"as "top managers and professionals—from lawyers to CFOs to consultants—who've been trained at top schools and companies and choose to pursue project-based careers independent of any major firm." Corporations are increasingly trusting individuals in these positions to do mission-critical work that in the past was done only by permanent employees or established outside firms. Supertemps are growing in number and are changing the way how business works. [7]

Many of my colleagues who hire contingent workers (part-timers, temps, interns, consultants, outsourced workers, and contractors) are also seeing a huge upswing in temporary positions. Some say that in the next 10 years, the contingent worker may be representative of the new normal workforce. One study conducted by Randstad revealed that 67 percent of senior executives plan to maintain "leaner" organizations by outsourcing work or hiring contract workers. As emergent workforce expert Carleen MacKay writes:

> The 21st century message is that if someone is not needed full-time, he or she won't be hired full-time. However, today approximately 30 percent of US workers are contingent workers. By 2020, according to a raft of experts—including Jeremy Neuner, CEO of NextSpace, a company that builds co-working communities—40-plus percent of American workers will be "freelancers" in all sectors of the economy. Other experts predict the number may be as high as 50 percent by 2020. Even if the 50 percent estimate is a little high for 2020, count on that number—or higher—by 2025.

> Freelancing is one way of defining the contingent workforce. Call them free agents, freelancers, temps, contractors, independent workers, just-in-time workers, or anything else—they are the workforce that is "contingent" on need. The main difference between some of the designations boils down to who markets the contingent worker. Is it an agency or the individual? Likewise, who pays the worker? Is it an agency or the organization?

The good news for these workers is that—unlike during the twentieth century—changing jobs is no longer a stigma, and, if properly positioned, a reasonably frequent job change demonstrates resiliency. In fact, we hear some hiring managers complaining that some workers "haven't changed jobs often enough," and, as a result, they question their current value. What a difference a decade or two makes!

A Changing Workforce

MacKay cites the following example of a typical 21st century contingent contributor's career journey within various organizational structures:

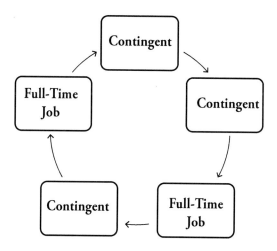

According to MacKay, the reason these workers will cycle between full-time and contingent work is "to keep pace with organizational, technological, and global changes that affect their status."

Businesses see that there is financial flexibility in having this type of workforce as contingent labor is cheaper and less risk. When bringing on temporary labor businesses do not have to provide them with benefits and there is no additional expense of workers compensation, payroll tax and burden of unemployment benefits. Temporary labor can be brought on and off assignment as needed.

More and more people are becoming "independent" or self-employed who may work directly with an organization instead of going through a staffing agency. In 2013, MBO Partners State of Independence Report confirms that independents are growing: "Independence is not a blip in the jobs economy, but a structural shift. The 2013 MBO Partners Independent Workforce Index, a measure created to track the sector, shows an 8.2% growth since the base year in 2011. Further, the independent workforce is expected to grow to 24 million strong by 2018." [8]

Finding Temporary Work

Given the benefits of working for a staffing agency, how do you find one? It's simple—just search the Internet, LinkedIn, Google, etc., or ask a friend.

Contact these agencies and find out what types of positions they place and companies they work with. A lot of staffing agencies specialize in placing workers in specific types of positions or fields, such as IT (information technology), accounting, administrative, light industrial, marketing, and C-Level (these are the "Chief" level positions such as Chief Executive Officer and Chief Technology Officer). If you feel that they are a good fit for you, go ahead and register with them. Be sure to follow up every couple of weeks. Many staffing companies offer skills testing, and it is advisable to take advantage of that opportunity.

Some staffing agencies may work with local companies that use what is called a VMS (vendor management system). With a VMS, companies (usually larger Fortune 500 companies) have a database of vendors (staffing agencies/recruiters) they use when they have job requisitions. Companies farm the requisitions to vendors that focus on specific categories, and staffing recruiters then submit candidates for those positions. Hopefully, the staffing agency will call you prior to submittal. If you are registered with multiple agencies, it's possible that you could be submitted more than once.

When you receive placement, keep a positive attitude and make sure you know what the company policies are regarding important aspects such as dress code. When your assignment ends, it never hurts to follow up with a thank you card to your manager. Carleen MacKay adds, "Prepare to ensure that your skills continue to match employers' requirements. Honor every contingent commitment by completing all assignments."

Have you ever thought about becoming an intern? A lot of intern positions today are not just for college students. This is increasingly something to be explored.

Portfolio Careers

Another option for today's worker is a "portfolio career," where you pursue more than one income source at the same time from different types of employment, such as part-time employment, temporary work, freelance assignments, and a personal business rather than a traditional full-time job.

In a *Forbes* magazine article titled "Portfolio Careers: Is the Latest Work Trend Right for You?" the author suggests that if you think you have the "right stuff," you should consider the following questions before jumping into a portfolio career:

- Do you multitask and manage your time well?

- Do you crave flexibility and creativity?

- Are you organized?

- Are you open to new opportunities?

Barrie Hopson, co-author of *And What Do You Do? 10 Steps to Creating a Portfolio Career*, notes that such careers offers a more fulfilling work-life blend, not to mention the economic safety provided by holding several different jobs. With a portfolio career, if you lose one job or choose to quit it, you will still be able to fall back on other sources of income. [9]

Strive not to be a success, but rather to be of value.
—Albert Einstein

To Do and/or Goals:

_____

_____

_____

_____

_____

8

Job Websites and Alerts

The way we search and apply for jobs has changed. We used to anxiously await the Sunday newspaper to look at the latest job listings, print out a résumé and mail it to a potential employer. Those days are long gone.

Today we can easily use smartphones to apply for a job within minutes. More companies are realizing the need to make websites mobile-friendly, thereby giving people looking for work easier access to apply for positions. Companies recognize our dependency on technology and are adapting to this reality.

Job Boards

First, a disclaimer: Using job boards should *not* be your primary means of looking for work! With this said, there are many valuable job-related websites in existence today. Some of the best ones that I have found are listed in Appendix C. In addition, there are sites such as Indeed and Simply Hired that aggregate job listings from thousands of websites, including company career pages, various other job boards, newspapers, and even state and federal job boards. It is also a good idea to search for professional organizations affiliated with your specialty, as these organizations may have a page on their website for companies to post positions.

Do not forget to explore federal, state, city, county, and school websites. Keep in mind that applying for a state or federal job is a usually a more detailed process and it might take a while to apply for just one job. To help ease the process, try to find someone in your area who has experience with applying for state or federal jobs. If you do opt to utilize job boards to upload your résumé, be sure to periodically review the information you have uploaded to ensure that it is current and that old versions of your résumé are not still floating around.

You don't want to spend all of your time scrolling through job boards, as it should be spent networking or making connections with companies where you want to work. So, to use your time wisely, create alerts on these job sites.

Alerts are emails sent to you when the site finds new results that match keywords that you have entered. The value of doing this is that it will save you those endless hours of searching job listings. You can then set aside time each day to review these alerts in your email.

To create an alert, simply go to one of the job sites on the Internet, set up keywords that relate to the type of position you want, and enter your e-mail address. An alert will then be automatically generated every time a specific keyword or term that you have entered appears on a website. Anytime a job is posted with that keyword, you will be notified by e-mail. Set up multiple alerts so that all of your keywords are in not in one alert.

Boolean Search

According to About.com, "Boolean searches allow you to combine words and phrases using the words AND, OR, NOT, and NEAR (otherwise known as Boolean operators) to limit, widen, or define your search. Most Internet search engines and Web directories default to these Boolean search parameters anyway, but a good Web searcher should know how to use basic Boolean operators."

I was first introduced to the Boolean search method when I started my career as a recruiter in the mid-nineties. It was one of the best ways my colleagues and I found candidates by using the Internet. As someone looking for work, you can use it too by searching jobs that companies post via their Applicant Tracking System (ATS).

Some of the larger ATS companies are Bullhorn and Taleo. You may have to experiment by using different keywords in combination with "and," "or," and your desired location.

Here's an example - searching for an accountant position in Los Angeles, go to Google and copy the following into the search bar: **site:bullhornreach.com/job**

intitle:"accountant" AND Los Angeles. This will pull up all companies that are using Bullhorn to post their jobs. You can do the same for Taleo: **site:taleo.net careersection:"accountant" AND Los Angeles**. Or, you can try typing this in: **site:taleo.net inurl:requisition:"accountant" AND Los Angeles**. Remember to bookmark your search, that way, you won't have to type it in again.

Yet another easier way to search ATS sites and their job listings is to go directly to www.bullhornreach.com/jobs.

Finding a job

When you find a job that you are interested in, do your research before applying. Go to LinkedIn first to find out who you know that works there and then contact them. They may be able to share with you more about the position and also contact the recruiter or hiring manager on your behalf. If do not know anyone directly at the company see if there is a 2nd or 3rd degree contact and reach out to the connection that you both know.

Google

In this day and age, you need to monitor your online reputation. You must know when people are posting things about you, especially if it's negative.

If you have never Googled yourself, you should do it. Oftentimes, recruiters and hiring managers will do a Google search to see what comes up about job candidates and prospective employees. Remember that nothing is ever *completely private* on the Internet and that any content you post on social media sites can be viewed by *anyone*.

For this reason, remember to be professional, engaging, and marketable when you post; you never know who might be checking you out. It is important to manage your online reputation.

Google Alert

Google has a free service called "Google Alerts" that can help you by notifying you whenever your name or something you are interested in is mentioned online.

Enter your name to serve as one alert, and then enter the companies where you are interested in working. Include information that relates to the type of work you are seeking. You can set up as many of these Google Alerts as you want.

Mark Anthony Germanos, social media director at YourSEOWizard.com, provides the following simple steps for setting up some alerts on key phrases[10]:

1. Go to http://alerts.google.com.

2. Click "Sign In" in the upper right-hand corner.

3. Sign in or create a new account.

4. Click the "Create a New Alert" button.

5. Type in a search query. This is the key phrase that you are targeting. It could also be your name, company name, or product name.

6. Choose a result type. I always choose "Everything."

7. Choose "How Often" you want to receive alerts. You can vary receipt of alerts from once a week to as-it-happens. The more sensitive the key phrase, the more often you would probably want the alerts. On the flip side, this could flood your e-mail inbox if you choose a popular key phrase and are sent alerts as they occur.

8. Choose "How Many" by selecting either "Only the Best Results" or "All Results."

9. Choose where Google should deliver the alerts. In the "Deliver To" pop-up, choose either your e-mail address or a feed. You can use Google Reader, which is also available at no cost, or fill in a feed reader you prefer. A feed reader functions like a table of contents. It shows you all the articles from multiple sources that meet your interest. A feed reader is a big time-saver.

10. Click the "Create Alert" button.

One of the alerts I have set up is for my name, "Melissa Washington." Not that long ago, I received an alert that a 19 year old Melissa Washington had been arrested in Florida. Luckily, the site also included her photo, which clearly was not me.

To Do and/or Goals:

_____

_____

_____

_____

_____

9

LinkedIn, Your Number One Tool

When it comes to networking and searching for jobs, LinkedIn is an even more valuable tool than Facebook or Twitter. LinkedIn is an outstanding platform that helps you exchange information, find resources, and search for career and business opportunities. At the time of this printing, LinkedIn has more than 300 million members worldwide —with two new members joining every second— and is the largest online professional network in the world. With that many members, what should you do to stand out?

Even if you are not looking for work (and 80 percent of LinkedIn users are not), LinkedIn can help you to connect with people, build your professional brand, and manage your contacts and database. LinkedIn provides the ability to build and control your personal online brand. Your LinkedIn profile is your online professional presence.

Unlike Facebook, you don't have to worry about "friends" tagging you in photos. LinkedIn is more professional and people interact differently than on Twitter or Facebook. Recruiters and hiring managers look on LinkedIn for talent to fill positions. Company applicant tracking systems (ATS) are increasingly now even allowing LinkedIn profiles to be imported.

Everything that I am sharing here pertains to the use of the free version which I feel is adequate for most users. There are upgrades specifically for job seekers, which are explained more at the end of this chapter. Listed below are the step-by-step tips on how to create a profile and best utilize LinkedIn for your professional purposes.

Settings and Primary Address

To create a LinkedIn profile, go to www.linkedin.com and register for an account. Once completed, click the "Account and Settings" tab at the top right of the page, under your photo (if you don't have a photo, the website will display a human shadow). From there, click the "Privacy and Settings" tab (you may be asked for your password) and then "Turn On/Off activity broadcasts." A box will pop up; I suggest unchecking the box as this will prevent your connections being notified via their newsfeed every time you make updates to your profile.

If you are using your work e-mail as your primary address, I highly recommend having a personal e-mail as a backup. The reason for this is that if you leave your current position for whatever reason and forget your password, and ask LinkedIn to send it to you it will be sent to your old work e-mail address, to which you no longer have access.

Profile

As previously stated, more recruiters than ever are using LinkedIn to fill job openings. For this reason, you should always have your professional profile current. It is important to have a completed LinkedIn profile that showcases your entire professional experience. Koka Sexton Sr., Social Marketing Manager at LinkedIn, emphasizes that, "Sales professionals, and really every professional, need to understand that their LinkedIn profile is *not* **their online résumé.** They simply need to take themselves out of that frame of mind. Your LinkedIn profile is really *your online brand,* your professional profile. It's really about the transformation in how you use your online persona, building your reputation by becoming a resource, and becoming that professional brand that draws people in." [11]

The more comprehensive your profile is, the more qualified you will appear to people who view it. In addition, you are 40 times more likely to come up in a search if your profile is complete. To make changes to your profile, go to "Profile" and click on "Edit Profile." You will know you are in edit mode when you see an object next to the items on the page that looks like a pencil.

It's important to list keywords that are specific to you several times throughout your profile. Think about what words you type in when you are looking for work or what words a recruiter would type in to find you. For example, if you are an accountant, your keywords might be "accountant," "Excel," "SAP," "general ledger," and "controller." Use synonyms, abbreviations, and full names. Be certain to have at least one of your keywords in your headline. If you are a military veteran, please make sure to use the word "veteran" multiple times throughout your profile, as some companies may specifically be looking for veterans to fill their positions.

Photo

Include a current, professional-looking photo of your face (important: you should be smiling). The photo should be only of you, so if your best photo is one with a pet or someone else, crop your companion out. Remember that LinkedIn is a professional environment; party photos and avatars are not a good fit. Your profile is seven times more likely to be viewed if you have a photo, and people may have an easier time recognizing and remembering you by your picture than by your name. If you are a military veteran, use a photo in which you are dressed in the attire for the job you want, not in your military uniform.

Your Professional Headline

Your headline, which appears below your name, is not your job title but your "tag line." To create this headline, consider what you would put on a billboard if you had one 120 characters to brand yourself. You want something that is going to differentiate you from the rest of the competition and make sure to have one or more of your keywords in your headline.

Remember that your headline is one of the first things people see when they do a search and that it shows up below your name in group discussions. So having a catchy headline could encourage someone to click on your profile. Think about how you provide value. Be specific. Who makes up your target market?

Another reason to have a good headline is when you apply through LinkedIn for a job, a short summary of your profile is sent along with your past three jobs and titles to the person who is hiring. A great way to stand out is to have a unique headline as it also appears under your name on status updates, group posts and in advanced search.

Location

LinkedIn works with geographical areas, so add your zip code. You can then choose to include either your specific city or greater metropolitan area. I recommend choosing your greater metropolitan area.

Primary Industry

Choose the primary industry in which you are interested from the drop-down list. If you cannot find one that is specific to you, choose the one that is the closest. This is where adding information in your summary will become important (see below).

Edit Contact Info

Under "edit contact info" add your Twitter handle if you have one. This way, when you share an update, you can tweet it at the same time. In addition, LinkedIn allows you to add three websites to your profile. To do this, click on the pencil next to websites (if you have something existing in there) or add websites. Choose the "Other" option, which will allow you to create a call to action in the next box by customizing the link. Instead of saying, "Personal Website," or "My Blog," choose "Other," and then enter a call to action that says, "Download My Résumé," or "View My Latest Blog Post." Copy and paste the website to which this will link.

Vanity URL

You can also create your own "vanity" URL. On your profile, there is a URL under your photo that begins, "www.linkedin.com/in/," is followed by your name and a bunch of letters and numbers, and has no Search Engine Optimization (SEO) value. Click on "Edit" after the URL, which will open another page that will take you to your public profile. Look for the link "Customize My Public Profile URL" and click on it. This will open up another box. Next, type in your first and last name in all lowercase letters with no spaces.

If no one has used that URL, you will get a green check mark, and then you can click on "Set Customized URL." If someone already has the URL, try entering your last name and then your first name, or put in a number after your name. Once you have created your URL, place the address on top of your résumé where you list your name, phone number, and e-mail address. You can also add this URL to your business cards, webpage, blog, and e-mail signature. This is a great way to demonstrate your professional and savvy social media abilities.

Public Presence

While you are on this page, you may notice that your profile looks different. This page shows your "public profile." When you create a LinkedIn profile, you create an online presence, which means anyone who is searching the Internet using Yahoo, Bing, Google, or any other search engines can view it. They don't have to be a LinkedIn member or be logged on to LinkedIn. It's your decision on how much you want to share with the public, but make sure to have your public profile visible to the public.

Summary Section

In the summary section of your profile, you have up to 2,000 characters to provide a personal story that will help employers remember you. Think of this section as your "virtual you," and add information that will make you stand out. Be wary of describing yourself in the third person as this gives off an impersonal feel. Write in the first person because it will give your summary a more genuine personal feel. While there will be a lot of *I*'s on your page, keep in mind that this is your profile and you are the one writing it. So when putting your summary together, write it as though you are looking through the lens of a "buyer" who is going to buy your product—you.

Experience Section

Next, add your experience by taking a few of the accomplishments from your résumé and expanding on them. Try to avoid making this section too similar to your bulleted résumé. Convey your successes, not your responsibilities. This is a great way to differentiate yourself from others who may have had similar experiences or background. Job Title there are 100 characters available.

To add your experience, make sure you are in "Edit Profile." Then click on "Add a Position." When you type in your company name, you will notice that it appears in a drop-down list. Choose the appropriate company. Once you save your selection, the company logo will appear on your profile.

You can include media links to enhance your profile such as a blog, YouTube videos, and news articles, and upload spreadsheets, Word documents, PDF documents, pictures, and presentations. Be sure to upload your résumé as either a Word or a PDF file. Use this opportunity to showcase your accomplishments and make sure not to post anything confidential.

Add your education, and be sure to include information about the schools you attended. Include any degrees you have earned, and highlight some of your activities.

A woman who came to one of my classes shared that she had received a call from a recruiter who said he needed her résumé ASAP. The woman was in the car with her family heading out for a vacation and did not have immediate access to it. However, she had taken my advice and uploaded her résumé to her profile, so she was able to tell the recruiter to simply go to LinkedIn and download it from there. This, in turn, landed her the job.

In 2013, LinkedIn published on its blog the "Most Overused Buzzwords of 2013": Responsible, Strategic, Creative, Effective, Patient, Expert, Organizational, Driven, Innovative, and Analytical. Don't go overboard on using them on your profile. LinkedIn shared a few best practices in its blog, for removing too-common buzzwords from your profile and creating a profile that is unique[12]:

1. Tie words to actual results – Instead of using weightless words, link your skills to specific results that demonstrate your competence.

2. Use active language – Rather than saying you are responsible for something, demonstrate how that responsibility delivered results.

3. Let others vouch for you – Seek out endorsements or recommendations from other reputable sources who can verify your talents.

Skills and Endorsements

In this section, list at least five skills and the specific expertise that you possess. These are the things for which people endorse you. Only list and accept the skills and expertise that you want to advertise.

Recommendations

Get at least two recommendations per position, as these will tell employers what you have accomplished far better than a résumé.

A good way to get a recommendation from a person is to provide them with one first. If you do so, the other person may be more likely to reciprocate. Always personalize the request that you send to people, and let them know exactly for what you are asking them to recommend you for. Remind them to make sure they spell-check their recommendations and if you receive a recommendation that has spelling or grammatical errors, decline it and send it back to be corrected.

Note that the person from whom you are requesting a recommendation needs to be on LinkedIn and a first-degree connection. You will need to have the position for which you would like the person to recommend you listed on your profile. Only request recommendations from people you know.

Other Sections

If you have received any honors or awards, list them. Add any other sections that apply, such as Volunteer Experience, Causes you Support, Test Scores, and Publications.

Seeing Who's Viewed Your Profile

On the free version of LinkedIn, if you have enabled your settings to show your profile to the public, you can view the last five people who have looked at it. You may notice that some people show up as "anonymous"—these individuals cannot see who has viewed their profiles. On the premium version of LinkedIn, you can see more than just the last five people who have viewed your profile. Seeing the people who view your profile can be a real morale booster. It's especially helpful when you have submitted a résumé for a position to know that someone from that company has looked at your profile.

Building Your Network

To build your network, start with people you know and trust, such as colleagues, customers, prospects, professors, alumni, people who served with, and supervisors. Work toward obtaining at least 500 first-degree connections. LinkedIn allows you to easily import contacts from e-mail accounts such as Yahoo, Gmail, Outlook, Hotmail, and AOL, so take advantage of this feature. You can also add connections one at a time by typing their names into "Advance Search." When the person you want appears in the search list, click on his or her name, and then click on "Connect."

Always customize the message that you send when making connection requests. Automated connection requests ("I'd like to add you to my professional network.") are generic and impersonal. It is important to take the time to personalize connection requests so you don't appear lazy. In addition, personalization keeps the "human" aspect in your request and provides the opportunity to share more information about yourself. Moreover, it will make you stand out. You have 300 characters to use in the invite and you cannot paste links or add attachments.

Take advantage of the opportunity these connection requests provide to let others know what you have been doing. It doesn't hurt to also let connections know that you are looking for work and would appreciate hearing about any opportunities that may arise. Be specific about the type of work you are seeking so you can avoid opportunities that are of no interest to you. Once again, this is why it's important to be clear about what you want to do and to develop a personal brand.

If you send a LinkedIn message to multiple people, make sure to uncheck the box that reads, "Allow recipients to see each other's names and addresses." This will ensure that you respect and maintain their privacy.

Whenever you meet people, try to connect with them on LinkedIn within 24 hours. Try to respond to an invitation or message through LinkedIn within one to two days. You can easily remove a connection and if you do, that person will not be notified that he or she has been "voted off your island." If you want to find your school alums, click on "Network" on the top bar and then "Find Alumni."

People You May Know

On your home page, to the right you will see a box labeled "People You May Know." Each time you log on to LinkedIn, this box will generate three new suggestions for connections based on commonalities you have with other connections. Remember, these are network generated possibilities, so you may or may not know these people.

Check Out Company Pages

You can explore different companies on LinkedIn by using the search bar at the top to type in the company name. On these company pages, you can learn specific information about a particular company, find people you know who work there, and/or find people you know who knows someone that works there. It's all about leveraging relationships. Be sure to check company pages prior to any interview, as they can provide useful information to help you identify questions to ask. Also, check out companies Showcase Pages for more information about them. There is also a "Careers" tab where companies list job openings.

Follow companies that you are specifically interested in working for, current employers, past employers, clients, vendors, and any other companies of interest. This will allow you to receive company updates on your news feed.

Searching for Jobs

Search for jobs that are posted on LinkedIn by employers. To do this, click on the "Jobs" tab in the top bar. Then type in your keyword in the job search box, but be sure to only search for one keyword at a time. Before you start clicking on the postings, make sure to hit "Save Search," which will be at the top right of the box, this will allow you to set up job alerts for each of your keywords and have a daily e-mail sent to you with postings that have each keyword either in the job title or description.

When viewing a job listing, you can often see who posted the job. Job posting's will show if the individual is a first-, second-, or third-degree connection, or an out-of-network connection. If this individual is a second-degree contact, it means you have a mutual contact. Reach out to the person you have in common, and ask for a referral or recommendation. Note that job postings may list your connections who work at that particular company, or they may list second- or third-degree connections.

To me, this feature is *gold* if you are looking for work, because it allows you to leverage the people you know to help you find your next career opportunity. With a name to contact, you no longer need to worry about sending your résumé to a "black hole". In addition, when looking at a company's job listings, remember to think about other people looking for work who might fit in advertised position. Pay it forward and send those openings to them.

Similar to the "People You May Know" section, LinkedIn has algorithms that use information to suggest "Jobs You May Be Interested In" or "Groups You May Like."

Sharing Updates

Share updates with connections via your home page. Some great things to share include the following:

- Links to articles that might interest your connections.

- Professional events you have attended or are going to attend.

- Specifics about the type of work you are seeking. For example:

  - Seeking a part-time position as an accountant in the Los Angeles area. (This shows you are being specific about the type of job and where you prefer it to be located. If you have a great headline this would pair nicely.)

  - Actively networking and researching opportunities with small- to medium-size health care organizations in Austin, Texas. (This one is also specific, but shows you are being active in your job search.)

Follow the "80/20 Rule" when it comes to sharing updates—make 80 percent of what you share about others and just 20 percent about yourself. Comment on or "like" the status updates your connections or the companies that you are following share, which are displayed in the "News Feed" tab on your home page. You never know when this might spark some interest. Remember that LinkedIn is not Twitter—it's all about the quality, not quantity, of posts. You can start slowly by adding an update once a week. Again, remember that updates posted on LinkedIn, can also be tweeted on Twitter.

Read what people in your network are reading and share relevant news information. Let your network know the type of work you are seeking. These are all great ways to keep yourself at the forefront of your connections' minds.

Joining Groups

Be a joiner! With more than one million groups on LinkedIn, there is sure to be something of interest to you. To find groups, find the tab labeled "Interests," which is the fifth one from the top of your home page. A drop-down menu will appear. Find and click on "Groups." You can also use the top search bar to look for groups that you may be interested in. Groups to look for could be company alumni, school alumni, personal interests, locations, military groups, job groups, and professional interests. Try to join at least 10 groups. If you don't like the group, you can always leave.

Look at other profiles to see what groups they belong to and if those may be worth joining. Feeling overwhelmed by the huge number of options? Don't worry—LinkedIn has great algorithms that will suggest groups that might be of interest.

Groups are a great resource for receiving career information, industry updates, event announcements, and job postings. You can follow members in a group in order to stay up-to-date on their information (note that "following" is different from "connecting" with a person). When I moved to Sacramento several years ago, I wanted to get more information about my new area, so I did a keyword search for "Sacramento" to join local groups. There were plenty of options for me to choose from. I strongly recommend joining Active Job Seekers of America group or other job seeker groups that are active in your area.

Make sure to participate in the groups you join, which not only will give you visibility but also will showcase your expertise. Take the initiative to comment proactively on others' discussions and share articles and job information. You can also easily copy a URL and paste it into a group discussion. Have good digital etiquette and be careful with posting negative comments. You would not want to post something that potentially could hurt you from getting a job.

Treat these groups as an opportunity to network with people with whom you normally would not have access. In fact, one of the greatest things about these groups is that they allow you to send messages to people you are not directly connected to. Just follow the same rules as above in posting updates to your groups.

For veterans, a great group to join is the Veteran Mentor Network. This group provides opportunities to connect with mentors and mentees.

Going Mobile

If you have a smartphone, download the LinkedIn app. You can easily search for companies, people and apply for positions listed on LinkedIn right from your smartphone. The app has lot of the same features as the online version. There is also a LinkedIn Job Search app that helps users find and apply for new jobs.

Managing Your Time

The most time you will spend on LinkedIn is when you first set up your profile, add connections, join groups, and set job alerts. Once you have completed these steps, you can better use your time staying engaged with companies and people in your industry, and keeping yourself at the forefront of their minds. Review your news feeds daily to see who has viewed your profile. When you do land a job, remember to update your profile.

Be mindful that depending on when you read this book, some of the functions listed for LinkedIn may have changed, as this platform does undergo periodic modification. LinkedIn also has useful FAQ pages, webinars, and customer service support if you have questions. Or, even better, you can contact me via LinkedIn. Finally, remember that although LinkedIn is a tool that will benefit you greatly when looking for work, it is not a solution in itself. It is still vitally important for you to make a human connection.

Job-Seeker Subscription

All the features discussed in this chapter so far are available on the free version of LinkedIn. With LinkedIn's Job Seeker subscription, you can rise to the top as a featured applicant, contact recruiters directly through InMail, and access the full list of "who's viewed your profile" (other than those who chose to remain anonymous).

Veterans, be sure to take advantage of special offers from LinkedIn. One of those is a free one year Job Seeker subscription. For more information, visit veterans.linkedin.com.

To Do and/or Goals:

_____

_____

_____

_____

_____

10

Get Social!

In today's market, it is essential to be social media savvy. Technology plays an increasingly critical role in the way we look for work, and sites such as Facebook, Twitter, Google+, Pinterest, and LinkedIn can serve as great resources to help you find your ideal position. Follow or "like" companies that interest you as well as specific people who work at those companies.

A Jobvite study found that 94 percent of employers use social media to recruit and 86 percent are likely to check out your online profiles once you apply to their job.[13] In my own experience, a number of recruiters I've spoken to say that they look for candidates by using platforms such as LinkedIn, Google+ and by checking out potential candidates' Twitter feeds and blogs. Some recruiters do not even ask for résumés at all, as they are able to find adequate information by using just these sites. As these examples illustrate, it is a smart move to establish a tasteful online presence with social media.

When setting up social media accounts, be consistent with the information that you use. Use the same photo across all platforms and link your profiles on each platform. Because LinkedIn is far and away the Internet's dominant job search, networking, and recruiting site, it is the sole focus on an entire section of this book (see chapter 9).

If after reading this chapter you still don't have a lot of clarity on these tools, I would recommend going to YouTube to watch a video on how to set up an account or search the internet for specific webinars on these platforms. I understand that sometimes it's easier to watch rather than read instructions.

Twitter

Twitter is a real-time source of information that has approximately over one billion registered users and over 250 million active users each month. When you communicate on Twitter, you send 140 character "tweets" through streams of ongoing conversation.

Create a free account on Twitter to showcase your professional profile. Start with constructing a bio (limited to 160 characters) that has relevant keywords which reflects your interests, and create a professional username, also called your "handle" (mine is @melissawashing) and add a photo of yourself so people can see you clearly.

Once you have set up an account, start following companies that interest you, and then start following specific people at those companies (recruiters, HR managers, career coaches, people in the department that you are interested in, etc.). Watch for tweets that alert you about job openings or upcoming networking events that can benefit your job search. You can also search the Twitter home page for tweets about specific companies, locations, and job titles. The first word to search would be "job." For better results, type in the hashtag symbol (#) before the keyword you are entering in. Twitter organically created this symbol (which I always knew as the pound sign) as a way to categorize messages.

Today, more employers are beginning to tweet jobs openings via Twitter or at www.tweetmyjobs.com. Employers may actually use Twitter to tweet about jobs for which they need to hire people quickly due to the real-time nature of the social network.

Post appropriate tweets, follow hashtags, and use hashtags when you tweet. Some hashtags you may want to follow include #jobs, #jobadvice, #careers, #résumés, #greenjobs, #freelance, and #personalbranding. To establish engagement with others on Twitter simply retweet or "favorite" a tweet. Once you set up your Twitter handle, add it to your LinkedIn profile (see chapter 9).

Facebook

Facebook is an online social networking service with over one billion registered users. You can connect and share content with your Facebook friends, in groups, and on others' Facebook pages. While many view Facebook primarily as a social tool, be aware that it is a serious professional tool used my millions as a place to find work and do business. A Facebook friend may share a job lead or you might find them in one of the groups you belong to. You should "like" companies and professional organizations that you are interested in, because they may post job leads on their Facebook pages.

When you set up your Facebook account be sure to review your privacy settings so that they reflect your comfort level and preferences. Facebook has some of the more complex privacy settings of the major social media sites, and these options change constantly. If you do share anything with the public, it should include your professional history, work experience, education, and professional skills. To find out more about this, visit: www.gcflearnfree.org/facebook101/1.

Blogs

Wikipedia defines a blog as a discussion or informational site published on the World Wide Web and consisting of discrete entries ("posts") typically displayed in reverse chronological order (the most recent post appears first). You may have heard it referred to as a diary or listing of journal entries that can be viewed by others on the Internet. It's easy to start one, and blogs give you an opportunity to showcase your expertise in a given area while building your social status online. A great site that gives you step-by-step guidance on how to build a blog is www. theblogstarter.com.

Google+

Google+ is a social media platform with over five hundred million active users. It is very different from the other platforms—yes, it involves online socializing, communicating, and people, but it also adds a social layer across the many services that Google+ offers. Relationship building is the one of the main factors for anyone to use Google+.

Having a presence on Google+ can shape what information is available about you online. If you already have a Gmail or YouTube account you already have a Google+ account. If not, go to plus.google.com to set up an account. In the "About" section of your profile share what type of work you are looking for. Add links to other social media platforms.

You can control what you want the "public" to see and what is seen within your circles. Your circles are friends, family, acquaintances and circles that you create and name. Add users directly into the appropriate circles and the different circles you can share specific interesting content appropriately within each circle. There is also a feature to "follow" users of your choice. Like the other platforms, it's important to "follow" or connect with hiring managers, career coaches, recruiters and others that can assist in your job search. This platform is a great place to post updates that showcase your knowledge in a specific area.

Additionally, by subscribing to anything Google-related, you also appear higher in the Google search rankings. Needless to say, this is a great platform to be on, especially if you don't have a website or blog.

YouTube

YouTube is a video-sharing website and currently the second largest search engine, right behind its owner, Google. On YouTube, create your own channel where you can post a video résumé to creatively promote yourself. Make sure to include a link to you LinkedIn profile so someone will have access to more information about you. What a great way to stand out from the competition.

Pinterest

Ninety-two percent of this site's users are women, but guys, don't let that scare you off! Pinterest is used to organize and collect a variety of online items that are of interest to the subscriber. Pinterest users "pin" items of interest from all over the Internet to different boards that they set up.

Being on Pinterest shows you can embrace new ideas and use valued social media platforms. But it's not all about recipes and home décor.

Set up your profile with a photo. In "About You" include a description of the type of work you are looking for and a link to your LinkedIn profile. You should only display your résumé on this site if it is visually appealing. This can be easily done by turning your résumé into an infographic. Showcase your experience and skills using pictures…. they say a picture is worth a thousand words.

Find and follow career experts, people, recruiters and companies you are interested in and pin content they have to your boards. Create a board with companies that are on your target list and include office locations and job positions that would be of interest to you.

Also set up a board that reflects you and your professional interests: quotes from you and others, professional organizations, events attended, community involvement, and so on.

Not ready to "pin" just yet? Follow these career-focused boards in the meantime: CareerBliss (www.careerbliss.com) and Careerealism (www.careerealism. com).

To Do and/or Goals:

_____

_____

_____

_____

_____

11

Volunteering

I highly recommend that you volunteer while you are looking for work. Doing so will not only build your self-confidence but will also strengthen your résumé. You never know what might open a door to a possibility you would never have considered or been aware of. Organizations are always looking for reliable people with great skills and volunteering allows you to network and highlight your talents while making a meaningful difference in your community.

Jim Carman the Director of Transition Center at Military Officers Association of America urges that we, "Accept the notion that obstacles placed in our path test our tenacity and our perseverance. Keep a positive attitude as you re-double your job search efforts and consider doing some volunteer work to add ballast to your résumé."

Find a place to serve, add that volunteer experience to your résumé, and be sure to discuss it when you land an interview. Sometimes, volunteer work can make all the difference when it comes down to you and another person competing for a job. Imagine if you were a hiring manager and two people came into an interview who both had a gap in their employment. One had been volunteering during this downtime, whereas the other had been sitting on the couch. Who would you choose?

You can find volunteer opportunities by searching on the Internet or by inquiring of local groups in your area, your kids' school, your church, rotary clubs, and Volunteers of America. You could also consider helping a charity with fundraising efforts. If money is tight, find charity work that you could do from home, or partner with someone so that you can share the driving. Our job-seekers group volunteered a couple of times at Meals on Wheels, where we helped prepare food for local seniors. It was such a great feeling to serve in this way. It was also pretty cool to shoot applesauce from a hose into little cups!

Jim Carman also notes that, "Organizations of all stripes need reliable volunteers with good people skills, financial acumen and attention to detail – the same qualities nurtured and refined during military service and in previous career roles. For specific volunteer ideas, start with the Corporation for National and Community Service at www.cns.gov (202-606-5000) and The Service Corps of Retired Executives at www.score.org (800-634-0245) with links to 348 local offices where volunteers with public and private sector experience are needed to assist small businesses and entrepreneurs."

Part of many company's culture includes giving back to the community, so why not be a candidate who stands out? Volunteering will give you those priceless feel-good moments that instill a sense of self-worth for having helped others. It will allow you to become a mentor or a mentee. It also has many other intangible benefits that you cannot quantify. And remember that when looking for an opportunity, volunteering is something you can continue even when you get back to work.

While I was looking for work I sought a volunteer opportunity that could include my daughter and that I could continue once I found a job. I found such a position where each week my daughter and I would go the local Panera Bread restaurant to pick up the unsold bread and baked goods and take it to the local transition shelter. It was a great experience for me and my daughter. Plus my car would smell really good.

Success is not about money you make, but about
difference you make in peoples lives .
—Michelle Obama

To Do and/or Goals:

_____

_____

_____

_____

_____

12

Your Résumé and Cover Letter

One day, the good old-fashioned résumé as we know it will fade into the sunset. Even today, many people are beginning to use their LinkedIn profile in place of a résumé (refer to chapter 9 for more information). However, there are still employers who ask for traditional résumés, so you will likely need one when you apply for a job.

If your résumé is not ready, don't let that stop you from looking for work. As Judy Isaman, a career development mentor, notes, "While a résumé is an important first step in moving forward in your career journey, knowing where you are and where you want to be is the precursor to job hunting or career creation."

Creating a Résumé

When you start to build your résumé, keep in mind that recruiters will, on average, spend less than one minute looking at it when doing an initial screen. Use the following tips in this chapter to create your résumé that presents you in the best possible light. I've reviewed thousands of résumés during my time as a recruiter and helping people look for work, and know what makes a résumé stand out.

Getting Ready to Write Your Résumé

Begin by gathering your past résumés, recommendations, evaluations, and reviews. Next, make a list of your skills, strengths, and professional achievements. Highlight your most marketable features that pertain to what type of work you are looking for. Show prospective employers what you did in your previous jobs and how that work benefited your company. Present clear examples and quantifiable statistics (by using dollar amounts, percentages, and numbers). Make sure to check the spelling and grammar. A word of caution: Don't rely on spellcheck, as it is not foolproof and will not indicate, for instance, when you have used the wrong word in a sentence. (For example, "I was the office manger at my last place of employment." See the mistake?) Strive for clarity and have a couple other people review it as well. Make your résumé understandable by avoiding jargon.

Résumé templates can be found on Microsoft Word and also by searching the Internet for "résumé templates." Don't forget to utilize local resources that can assist you with putting your résumé together (see chapter 2).

Components of a Successful Résumé

Here are the elements needed to create an effective résumé:

1. *Personal Information:* At the top of the page, include your name, professional e-mail address, phone number (use your cell phone number, unless you have a trusted person who would answer your home number), and LinkedIn profile URL (make sure your public profile is visible; see chapter 9 for more information). Your street address is not needed.

2. *Personal Statement:* The traditional "objective statement" is now considered passé. This place on your résumé should instead be used to provide a personal summary that includes your branding statement. It should articulate what is important to you as it relates to the position, as well as what you have to offer. The purpose of the summary is not to list what you are looking for but, to tell the prospective employer why you are an ideal candidate for the position. When crafted well, this section should make a potential employer

want to continue reading.

3. *Experience:* Include your previous work and/or military experience and list the names of the organizations for which you worked, their locations, and dates of employment. A chronological format is usually best, though in certain situations—such as if you are transitioning into a new field or are reentering the workplace—a functional résumé may be more appropriate. List your most recent work experience first, and use bullet points to highlight key accomplishments. Create content that is SMART—Specific, Measurable, Achievable, Results-Oriented, and Time-Bound.

4. *Education and Training:* List the schools you attended, the dates attended, and the academic degrees and honors earned. Also list any special training you received. This section may need to go before the "Experience" section depending upon the type of position you are applying for.

5. *Volunteer Work:* List any charitable organizations for which you have volunteered your time to serve. You may also want to consider listing your volunteer work under the "Experience" section instead of categorizing it separately, especially if it is connected to what you have been doing or want to do. Consolidating this information under "Experience" is a good rule of thumb if you have been out of work for a while (see chapter 11).

6. *Awards and Achievements:* List any special awards or honors you have received if they are pertinent to the position for which you are applying. These types of achievements will help you stand out.

7. *Skills:* List any technical skills you possess (e.g., computer programs you know, special knowledge you have, languages you can speak, etc.).

8. *Professional Associations:* List any associations you have joined and what you did at those associations if they relate to the job for which you are applying.

A good rule of thumb to follow is to have one page in your résumé for every seven to 10 years of relevant work experience. Limit the total experience you cover to 10-15 years, as long as it's still relevant. Don't wordsmith your statements to death and use action-driven phrases. Remember, you want to grab recruiters on the first page. Job coach Diana Conwell suggests that you think like an employer when developing your résumé:

> Job seekers make the mistake of thinking they need to stack up every detail of every job they ever did on their résumé. I call this the "résumé novel," and it makes for an unnecessarily long and difficult-to-read document. Hiring officials today do not have time to read them, and they don't have to do so, because there are plenty of other applicants to choose from. So instead, *think like a hiring official when you write your résumé.* Hiring officials are only interested in what you can do for their job and whether you have the skills and personality to do it. They are less interested in where you worked before and more interested in how you work and what you can do, regardless of where you got your skills.

If you lack experience in a specific field, or if you are applying for an entry-level job, add as much experience and education as you can. Make sure to include any volunteer work or specific training. Avoid including personal information such as home address, date of birth, place of birth, social security number, and blood type. It is also not necessary to state that "references are available on request." Employers expect that you have references, so you don't need to waste your valuable résumé space making this statement.

Transitioning from Military Service

If you are transitioning out of the military, remember to de-jargon your résumé and turn your skills and experience into terms that civilians can understand. There are excellent resources available that can help you do this, such as:

- Feds for Vets (mst.vaforvets.va.gov/mst/va/mos-translator)

- Military OneSource (www.militaryonesource.mil/transition)

- Nrd.gov

- O*NET OnLine (www.onetonline.org)

- Transition Assistance Program (www.taonline.com/TAPOffice)

- Additional Veteran resources can be found in Appendix D

Customizing Your Résumé

Once you have completed your résumé, it will serve as a generic template that you will likely want to customize each time you apply for a job. Every time you submit your résumé, you will need to modify it to include specific keywords and accomplishments that are directly related to the job for which you are applying. One size does not fit all when it comes to résumés; the most effective ones are those that are targeted to a specific position.

An excellent way to determine if you have all the keywords for a job in your résumé's profile is to do a word cloud. A word cloud is visual picture of text where the size of the word indicates its importance. These can be done for free. Go to Google and type in "word cloud." Several sites that generate word clouds will appear. Wordle is a good one to use (www.wordle.net). Copy the job description and place it into the website, which will then create your word cloud. In the example below, I used my bio, which I copied and pasted into a word cloud program. These were the results it produced:

Saving, Formatting, and Tracking Your Résumé

When you save your résumé as a Word, PDF, or .txt file, title the file name with your name and the job position for which you are applying. This will help the recruiters as they often receive hundreds of résumés each day. When you apply online through a company's website, you will be submitting your information to their Applicant Tracking System (ATS, also known as Talent Management Systems), which help recruiters/HR manage the entire recruitment process, so it's important to format your résumé correctly. Include keywords, as these tracking systems are programmed to search résumés that contain these phrases. Do not include italics, underlined words, tables, images, accent marks or text in the header and footer, as these will scramble your information in the tracking system. Also use compatible "conservative" fonts, such as Arial, Tahoma, Verdana, Calibri, and Book Antiqua. Don't use a font size smaller than 11 points, and keep a one-inch margin on the top and bottom of your document. When using bullets, keep it simple and avoid decorative shapes.

It is important to have a trusted colleague review your résumé and provide candid feedback. Remember that résumés are subjective, so everyone will have a different opinion about what makes one more effective than another.

Untraditional Résumé Approach

As noted earlier, the paper résumé will eventually fade into the sunset. So in addition to creating a LinkedIn profile, build a visual résumé. You want to stand out in the crowd and many recruiters out there are tired of seeing the same old résumés over and over. Visual types of résumés are becoming increasingly popular. Sites such as Vizualize.me (www.vizualize.me) and VisualCV (www.visualcv.com) are worth exploring. As with LinkedIn, these sites allow you to upload videos, add photos and post links to other sites.

How about changing it up a little and creating an infographic-style résumé? If you don't want to get that fancy, create your résumé visually in PowerPoint. Tell your story on slides and then upload it to www.slideshare.net, which is a platform for PowerPoint presentations. (Think of it as the YouTube of PowerPoint.) This will also help you gain more visibility. I created a PowerPoint while I was looking for work back in 2010 with my title, "Who is Melissa?" I used pictures and logos to tell my story; it is still on slideshare if you want to take a look.

These non-traditional approaches can be viewed as tools to complement your traditional résumé.

Biography

Jim Carman from the Military Officers Association of America (MOAA) shares why a biography might be needed to support your job search.

> If you are a more senior person who has held a variety of roles throughout your career, it's an excellent way of painting a coherent picture of yourself to someone other than a potential employer. While a résumé screams "I'm looking for a job," a biography is a softer-sell that can be used to introduce yourself to a networking contact or as a read-ahead for a meeting or engagement with someone whom you may not know well.

> What you choose to include depends on what you want to accentuate and how you want to be perceived by those who are reading it.

> It's considered best practice not to burden your reader with lengthy sentences of personal information unless it applies directly to the subject for which the biography has been prepared. It's also an acceptable opportunity for shameless self-promotion.

Carman also shares some best practices for developing a biography:

- Photographs are not recommended.

- Don't hide your military experience by using civilian job titles.

- Avoid excessive acronyms and jargon.

- Write in the third person voice using a conversational tone. A common and effective format is:

    - First Paragraph: Connect with your reader or audience by highlighting a major career achievement. Include your name and current or former professional title.

    - Second Paragraph: Describe some of your proudest accomplishments from throughout your work history. Shift to referring to yourself in first name only.

    - Third Paragraph: Emphasize special skills and strategic connections that could have significance with the reader.

    - Fourth Paragraph: Validate your achievements by citing educational credentials and business-related honors.

Creating a Cover Letter

Once you have your résumé in place, you need to draft a cover letter. This letter basically tells prospective employers why they should read your résumé. Drafting this document can be difficult, and there is a 50/50 chance that recruiters will never read it. However, it's always best to error on the side of caution—you do not want a recruiter to put your résumé in the "no" pile because you did not include a cover letter. Even if the job description does not ask for it, include one anyway.

Read through the job description as it may have additional requirements that the recruiter may be using to screen candidates. They may ask you to submit a video or design a flyer for the position or respond to a specific problem. This takes a little extra effort but take the time to do it well because it will help you stand out.

Getting Ready to Write Your Cover Letter

For each résumé you submit, you should also submit a corresponding cover letter. When drafting your letter, approach it more as writing a simple letter to the hiring manager than as composing a formal letter. The goal is to capture the reader's attention in a straightforward manner. Write in your voice and try to keep the letter to one page. A good place to start is to use a template from Microsoft Word. When you are in Word, go to "New" and type in "Cover Letter." There are several different templates from which to choose.

Components of a Cover Letter

Here are the essentials you need to include to create an effective cover letter:

1. *Date:* Type in today's date.

2. *Heading:* Type the name of the hiring person (if known), the company name, and the company address.

3. *Body:* Begin by stating where you found the position and why you are qualified for it. Take the time to review the job requirements in the posting and the important skills that are referenced. Share a specific example not listed on your résumé to show how your experience matches up with something from the job description.

4. *Closing:* Express your interest in the position and the company. State something specific about the organization by referencing an article that you saw about it. Thank the person for taking the time to review your résumé, and then request an interview. State specific times and dates when you will call to arrange an interview (allow at least three business days from the day you send the letter).

5. *Signature:* Include your name and contact information (your e-mail and phone number).

You want to catch the hiring manager's attention, as they will probably be receiving a large response to the job posting. In addition, like your résumé, once you have a cover letter in place, use it as a template to draft future cover letters.

Submitting Your Cover Letter and Résumé

When submitting your cover letter and résumé via e-mail, make sure the subject line will get the recipient's attention. Include the title of the job in the subject line, copy and paste the information into the body of the e-mail, include a link to your LinkedIn profile, attach your résumé, cover letter and any other pertinent documents. Keep your e-mail brief and friendly, and remember to thank the person who is reviewing your application for their time.

Another way to stand out from the crowd is to also mail your résumé and cover letter in addition to e-mailing them. Put the unfolded documents in an 8" x 11½" flat white envelope. A slight downside to this approach is that the hiring manager might need to scan the cover letter and résumé into the company's system, and having something electronic will make it easier for him or her to forward and register it in the company's Applicant Tracking System. If you do mail your documents, either mention that you have sent them electronically, or include the documents on a flash drive in the envelope.

Following Up

I recommend following up within two to three days with the person to whom you submitted your résumé via e-mail or phone. This will show that you have serious interest in the position. Also, the person that you had sent it to may have not received it or it was "lost" in their inbox. Much of the difficulty with calling is that you may not have a phone number. If you follow up, the best time to reach the individual is usually first thing in the morning. Be prepared either to speak to the individual or to leave a message and know in advance what you are going to say.

When you call and the hiring manager happens to pick up, say something such as, "Hello, this is (your name) I recently submitted my résumé for the (position for which you are applying). I am calling to confirm that you received it, and I wanted to ask you a few questions." Be ready with your questions. Good questions include, "Have you had a chance to review my résumé? What kind of experience does an ideal candidate have? What are the biggest challenges I would face in this position? When are you scheduling interviews? Can we schedule one right now?" (If you are going to ask this last question, have your calendar in front of you.)

To Do and/or Goals:

_____

_____

_____

_____

_____

13

The Interview

Once you've made it to the interview process (either via phone or in person), the potential employer has obviously seen something in you and is interested in knowing more. Many times, the interview just gives the potential employer a chance to determine whether you will be a good fit for both the position and the organization.

When you think about the interview process, you will likely start to get nervous. There are two things that can help you prepared physically and mentally. First, be sure to exercise and get enough sleep (see chapter 1). A good night's rest the night before an interview is important so that you look fresh and alert. Mentally, know what is coming. Be prepared with information about the company, anticipate questions, and have the answers. After reading through the information in this chapter, you should be ready.

I'll let you in on an insider tip . . . Want to really *wow* them? . . . Put together a PowerPoint presentation!

Conducting Preliminary Research

Before the interview (whether it is via phone or in person), research the company and the person with whom you are interviewing. This will put you in a better position to answer questions. Many recruiters have shared with me that they are amazed at how many people *do not* prepare for interviews.

There are several places to conduct research and learn more about prospective employers. Here are some of the best online resources to explore:

1. Company website: Begin by visiting the website of the company to which you are applying.

2. Yahoo Finance and Google: Visit these sites to find relevant news pertaining to the company. Gather information on the company's annual report, current stock price, and recent trending articles.

3. Glassdoor: Search through a huge database of company reviews, office photos, CEO approval ratings, and more.

4. Vault: Get inside scoop on companies.

5. LinkedIn: View the company's profile on LinkedIn.

6. Indeed.com/forum: Job interview tips posted by professionals and job seekers

Be sure to research the person with whom you will be interviewing with prior to the meeting. You can find most people on LinkedIn and learn how long they have been at their respective companies, their titles, the previous companies at which they worked, groups they have joined, what companies they follow, what influencers they follow, see who you know in common, and what their career paths are. If the person interviewing you has a unique name, it is always a good idea to learn the correct pronunciation. Attention to details like this does not go unnoticed and work toward creating a positive first impression of you.

Preparing Answers to Questions

Be sure to anticipate what questions the interviewer will ask and how you will respond. Be ready with specific examples to share because they are much more effective than generalities. The following questions are typically asked by employers:

- Are you a team player?

- Have you ever had a conflict with a previous manager, and, if so, how was that conflict resolved?

- How can you add value to this organization?

- How did you hear about this job?

- If I were to ask a previous boss to describe you, what would he or she say?

- What are your strengths?

- What are your weaknesses?

- What can you tell me about yourself?

- Where do you think you will fit in best in this organization?

- Why did you leave your last job?

The interviewer may also ask behavior-based questions that will require you to cite specific examples and experiences. These typically begin with the statement, "Describe a time when. . ." Recruiters like to ask these questions because past performance is a predictor of future performance. Jeff Dunn, campus relations manager for the Intel Corporation, offers the following advice on how to best answer behavior-based questions:

> The task of trying to come up with good examples off the top of your head is one of the biggest sources of stress before and during an interview. The solution is to prepare some "success stories" prior to the interview. Sketch out some stories in a situation-action-result format that you could apply to multiple questions. The stories could illustrate major accomplishments, things you completed that had a measurable outcome, things you are most proud of, and certainly a time you adeptly handled an angry customer, boss, or co-worker.

As an example, Dunn notes that students with little work experience, can say, "I led a class project team of four in building a robot. One class member dropped out mid-term and I reorganized the work between the three of us. We completed the project on time and got an A." This story could be used to respond to questions about teamwork, meeting deadlines, and flexibility.

Preparing Questions to Ask

In addition to answering questions adeptly, you can really impress the interviewer by asking good and probing questions. Try to ask as many questions as the interviewer. The recruiter has likely heard similar responses from many applicants, so your goal should be to make "your pitch" as to why you are the best candidate for the job. Remember that you are also interviewing them to see if they are a good fit for you. Some questions to ask include:

- How would you describe your management style?

- What are some examples of projects that I may be working on?

- What are you seeking in the ideal candidate for this position?

- What are your expectations for the first thirty to ninety days?

- What do you see as the biggest challenges in this position?

- What is the company's vision? What are its plans for growth and stability?

- What resources are available?

- What would be my daily responsibilities?

- Why is this position open?

The *most important* question to ask is to ask for the job. If you want the job, you need to ask for it! This is often one of the hardest parts of the interview, and most interviewers won't be expecting it, so you may catch them off guard. Below are some examples of follow-up questions. Pick one that you are most comfortable asking:

- Do you see anything that would prevent you from making me an offer?

- How do I rank in comparison to other candidates you have interviewed for this position?

- How do you see me fitting in with your company?

- Is there any reason I'm not fully qualified for this position?

Do a practice interview with someone you know and go through each of these questions. It's important to understand that the company should be a place where you will enjoy working and in line with your values. Think about and write down your personal values prior to the interview. When you're looking for work, it is easy to become so desperate that you feel you must take any position just because it's a job. For this reason, it's important to take the time to research the company. There is nothing worse than starting a position and realizing that it is not for you. This can make you feel disengaged, and you may end up quitting or getting fired.

Be aware that an assessment may be given before an interview. Many companies use assessments to determine if you are the right fit for the position and company and come in many different formats including video games. There is really no way to prepare for these assessments as they are not a "test". When I worked in staffing we administered a test called "Wonderlic" which was more of an IQ test and this is the same test that is given to potential NFL pro football draft picks.

One to Two Days Before the Interview

The day before your interview, e-mail the person who is going to interview you to confirm the time and location. At least two days before, drive by the location if you can to estimate how long it will take to get there and will give you a better idea of the area.

The Day of the Interview

Once you've finally made it to the big day, there are several things to be mindful of to give yourself the best opportunity for success.

Phone Interview

If asked to interview by phone, try to schedule a time when you will not have any distractions. If using a cell phone, make sure you are in an area with good reception. Turn off any music or the TV, as the background noise can be disrupting. Don't eat while you are on the phone, and definitely don't be driving. Find a place where you can have all of your research and your résumé readily accessible and are able to take notes. If you have call waiting and a call comes in on the other line, do not to answer it. Phone interviews require the same level of professionalism as in-person interviews.

Web Interview

The same guidelines for phone and in-person interviews apply to web interviews. For web interviews you will need to have a web cam. I would recommend checking out sites commonly used during Web interviews—such as Skype, Google Hangouts, WebEx, and GoToMeeting—to become more familiar with them if you aren't already.

In-Person Interview

It is very important to make a positive first impression during the interview process. Before leaving your home, take a good look at yourself in the mirror. Smile. Rehearse what you are going to say. This will give you more confidence during the interview.

Dress to Impress

Dress appropriately, and make sure you are presentable before you walk in the door for your interview. Make certain that your hair is combed, your nails are nicely groomed, your clothes are ironed, your breath is fresh, and you smell good (don't overdo it on the perfume, though). Remember to smile! If you are a smoker, try not to smoke before your interview. Leave the coffee cup in the car. Bring copies of your résumé, the job description, your company research, a pad of paper, and a pen.

A quick story illustrates the importance of what's stated above an office where I once worked had windows on the first floor that looked right out onto the parking lot. One day, I watched as a guy in his car shaved, tweezed his nose hairs, and brushed his hair. When he got out of his car, he used one of those stick rollers to get all the lint off of his suit. Of course, I did not say anything to him when he was sitting across from me during the interview, but he could clearly see his car from where we were sitting. The lesson: be cautious of what you do in your car in front of the building where you will be interviewing. Again, do your preparation at home.

Invest in a nice suit and shoes or even just a nice blazer and slacks. Ladies, it is not appropriate to show cleavage and/or midriff in an interview. Thrift stores are a great resource to find some nice clothing at reasonable prices—just make sure to have them dry-cleaned. If you are a military veteran, don't wear any parts of your uniform. That means you must leave the chloroforms at home. I wish I had a camera on the day a candidate came in wearing her slippers. When I asked why she was wearing them, she told me she did not know she was coming in for an interview.

Keep an extra tie or blouse in your car just in case you spill something on yourself before your interview. Remember that you don't get a second chance to make a good first impression!

When to Arrive

Be punctual and arrive 10 to 15 minutes early. Use the time while you are waiting to ask the receptionist or security guard about the company and what it is they like about working there. Treat everyone you meet with respect and courtesy. The receptionist may not be conducting the interview, but his or her opinion may be solicited. Get a feel for the environment and the interaction between the staff. Don't forget to turn off your cell phone before you go into the interview.

Don't be late, as arriving late makes you seem unreliable and rude. If an unforeseen circumstance arises and you must be late, do everything you can to call ahead.

What to Bring

Bring a generic "master application" that you have already completed to reference when filling out the application for the position. Although application styles and content vary, this will make it easier to recall information requested on the form. Follow the directions carefully, complete all the fields, double-check everything and don't volunteer unnecessary information. For reference a sample master application is included in Appendix E.

Bring multiple copies of your résumé, in case the interviewer forgot it or brings in someone else for you to meet. Also bring a few business cards and three printed references (include your references' names, phone numbers, e-mail addresses, and where you worked together). Your reference list should contain people who know your work performance, such as former bosses, colleagues, vendors, and clients. Contact your references prior to the interview to let them know that someone may be calling. They should know that you are looking for work and plan to use them as references; don't put them on the spot at the last moment.

During the Interview

When the interview begins, be ready with your questions and don't bash your previous employer. Use this opportunity to learn more about the company. Steer clear of answering illegal interview questions that pertain to your religion, age, gender, race, sexual orientation, and national origin. Listen to the interviewer and take time to answer questions, but do not take too long. Respond thoroughly but concisely. If you have gaps in your employment, be prepared to explain them. And again, when wrapping up, be sure to ask for the job.

Stay positive, smile, maintain eye contact, and have a good sense of humor. A CareerBuilder study conducted by Harris Interactive actually found that a candidate's sense of humor and involvement in his or her community ranked the highest in determining which candidates were hired.[14] Although you understandably might be somewhat nervous, try not to be tense during the interview.

Some companies like to interview candidates in a panel format. This is where you interview with more than one person at a time. When interviewing in this format, try not to focus on just one person.

One of the most difficult questions to ask or answer is about the salary you would like to receive in the position. Some good ways to respond are to say, "I am more interested in the role itself, rather than the pay," "I would expect to be paid the appropriate range for this role based on my years of experience," or even better, "Based on research, (insert range of pay here) is what I understand this type of position would pay." When you consider the position, factor in other benefits such as health insurance, dental insurance, vision insurance, a profit-sharing plan (a 401k with an employer match, for instance), stock options, bonuses, education assistance, paid parking, paid vacation time (what are the stipulations—use it or lose it?), paid sick time, holiday time, flex time, training, career development, and telecommuting. Remember to look at total compensation, not just the base salary. Good places to research are Salary.com, Glassdoor.com and professional organization websites.

After the Interview

Whether your interview was conducted over the phone or in person, send a handwritten thank you note to your interviewer and cite specifics from the interview. If there is something you forgot to address during the interview, bring it up in the note. It doesn't hurt to follow up with a phone call or e-mail—just remember that you may not get a response. This should be done if you are applying for a position internally as well.

I keep a box of stamped thank you cards in my car so I can write one up immediately following an interview. If there is something specific on which you connected with your interviewer or that you may have noticed this person had hanging in their office, then make the effort to get a specialized thank you card. For example, maybe you noticed that the person who interviewed you is a Disney fan. Go to the local store and find a Disney-themed thank-you card. One of the job seekers in our original group, Keith Roswald, had a nice selection of photographs, each of which he would in turn make into a personalized thank-you card. So, for instance, if he noticed the interviewer liked horses, he would use one of his photographs of horses. Remember, it's important to differentiate yourself!

To Do and/or Goals:

14

Starting Your Own Business

Have you ever thought of creating a second career in this new economy? Is there something you love doing that you think you can develop into a business? Do you possess the skills to do that job? Do you have support from your family and friends? Are you ready to take the financial risk? If so, you might be ready to launch a small business.

Different ways to start a business are: starting from scratch, buying an existing business or buying a franchise. Find out what works best for you and your current situation.

According to Cari Vinci of FranNet West (franchise consulting service), running your own small business requires a strong work ethic, discipline, persistence, self-confidence, and persuasiveness. There are also seven personality "quirks" that entrepreneurs share:

1. You see yourself as being unique.

2. You see a better way to improve everything.

3. You are easily bored.

4. You don't like rules.

5. You become immersed in projects.

6. You resist the status quo.

7. You have a burning desire to create.

If characteristics and qualities match your personality, you might want to consider striking out on your own. As Vinci states, "It's an adventure, a privilege, and incredibly rewarding to live your own dream."

If you do decide to take the plunge, you first need to decide what type of business you want to start. Do you want employees? Will you need office space? Do you need to develop a business plan? Will you need to borrow money? What about a franchise? Are you a veteran? (There are specific resources for vets.)

It's scary to go out on your own, but there are many resources available to help you get started, and many organizations that offer workshops. Two sites to explore such options are the Small Business Administration (www.sba.gov) and SCORE (www.score.org). Find your niche and get really good at it.

To Do and/or Goals:

_____

_____

_____

_____

_____

Conclusion and Encouragement

Hopefully, you found something within these pages that you can apply to your job search today. During my journey, I reinvented myself and found a way to use my passion for helping others. It started with holding free LinkedIn workshops at my dining room table for people looking for work. I found a niche in the marketplace that I could fill and one that I enjoyed. I built on my training and relationship-building skills and developed and refined them until I became known as an "expert."

One day, I had an "aha" moment and realized that I should start my own business that would allow me to utilize my strengths and skills. Using my passion to help others, I found what I love to do and did it, even when I was not financially compensated for it. It made it even better, of course, when I was able to find a way to get paid for what I love to do.

The path to starting my own business was quite a journey. I built my own website, completed paperwork to become a California-certified small business, and created flyers for the LinkedIn classes I had already been teaching at the local community college. Then I created a LinkedIn company profile. Not long thereafter, LinkedIn sent me an advertising credit.

I used this credit to place a pay per click (ppc) ad on LinkedIn that was targeted to a specific demographic in the Sacramento area, where I wanted to establish my business. Soon after that, I received a message from Nate Bride, who was director of sales effectiveness at LinkedIn. It just so happened that he lived in a neighboring city and had seen my ad. We met for coffee and stayed connected on LinkedIn.

In June 2011, I sent Nate a follow-up e-mail. He replied back and wanted to know if I would be interested in a three-month assignment working on planning internal event programs for LinkedIn sales trainings. Who would have thought the timing of my e-mail would have been so perfect? I started later that week.

Later that month, I was in Toronto with LinkedIn, coordinating its marketing solutions sales training. A couple of weeks after that, I was in the San Francisco Bay Area, assisting LinkedIn with its global hiring solutions training. I continued working on my business, although keeping busy with LinkedIn allowed me to focus more on helping people looking for work than gaining new paid clients.

By October of that year, I was visiting seven hotels in one day in Las Vegas, looking for a location for LinkedIn's Global Sales Kickoff that was to take place in January of the following year. Since that time, I have flown around the world planning events.

In addition, I have expanded my training business to include teaching organizations how to effectively use LinkedIn. Continuous focus on my niche has allowed me to become really good at it, which has also helped my marketing plan. My market has grown from the Sacramento to the entire globe. And because of my experience in the recruiting and events industries, I have been able to leverage existing relationships to further expand my profitable business.

This, in turn, has led to speaking engagements, which I never would have thought would happen. I was even featured on local Sacramento news station KCRA 3 (NBC) in a segment about using LinkedIn, in which the news anchor referred to me as "Lord of LinkedIn!"

And then, of course, I put this book together. This was a stretch for me—as many people know—because I do not like to write; I prefer brief, straight-to-the-point e-mails. In fact, one of the reasons I did not go back to earn an MBA was because of the writing I would have to do! But now I have surpassed even my own expectations and just written a book. It is amazing what doors open up and what you can accomplish if you just put your mind to it.

I sincerely hope the tips, tools, and resources I've shared will help you find your ideal job or career path. Don't be afraid of what others might think. As I often say and wholeheartedly believe, Dream big and live it!

All our dreams can come true, if we have the courage to pursue them.
—Walt Disney

Acknowledgements and Endnotes

I wanted to thank the folks that made a direct contribution to my book:

Cari Vinci, chapter 14

Carleen MacKay, chapter 7, 12

Diana Conwell, chapter 1, 2, 12

Ian Pamplona (cover)

Jeff Dunn, chapter 13

Jim Carman, chapter 3, 11, 12

John Quinn, chapter 2

Judy Isaman, chapter 3 & 12

Nicki Crapotta, chapter 1

Tony Restell, chapter 10

Special thanks to my fabulous editors, Cherise Henry and Jim Richardson. Thank you to Bill Carpentier, a fellow self-publisher who took the time to share with me the ins and outs. Thank you to Nate Bride for connecting with me and helping to change the course of my life.

A special shout out to the first members of Active Job Seekers of Roseville who put together that "I got a feeling" video. Appreciate your continued friendship- Michelle Thomas, John Quinn, Keith Roswald, Darrielle Ehrheart and Steven Lease.

Endnotes

Chapter 3

1 Tom Peters, *Brand Called You*, (Fast Company 1997), www.fastcompany.com/28905/brand-called-you

2 Graham poses this question in his book *Identity: Passport to Freedom.*

Chapter 4

3 ABC News, March 2012 http://www.recruitingblogs.com/profiles/blogs/80-of-today-s-jobs-are-landed-through-networking

4 Motto trademark is pending.

Chapter 6

5 Jessica Dickler, *The hidden job market* (CNN Money Reports, 2009) money.cnn.com/2009/06/09/news/economy/hidden_jobs/

Chapter 7

6 Employment News Brief, Randstad Workforce 360 Annual Report, September 9, 2012, http://www.randstadusa.com/workforce360/jobs-the-economy/employment-news-brief/27.

7 Jody Greenstone Miller and Matt Miller, *The Rise of the Supertemp*, (Harvard Business Review, May 2012), hbr.org/2012/05/the-rise-of-the-supertemp.

8 MBO Partners State of Independence Report, September 2013 www.mbopartners.com/mbo-partners-state-independence-report-reveals-independents-are-self-employed-successful-satisfied

9 *Portfolio Careers: Is the Latest Work Trend Right for You?* (Forbes, February 27, 2013), http://www.forbes.com/sites/learnvest/2013/02/27/portfolio-careers-is-the-latest-work-trend-right-for-you.

Chapter 8

10 Mark Germanos, *Why You Need to Use Google Alerts as Part of Your SEO Strategy*, (Examiner.com, July 30, 2012), http://www.examiner.com/article/why-you-need-to-use-google-alerts-as-part-of-your-seo-strategy.

Chapter 9

11 Koka Sexton, Sr., *Your Top Questions on "Social Selling" Answered by LinkedIn, Evernote, and Hubspot* (Hubspot February 20,2014) //blog.hubspot.com/marketing/questions-social-selling-answered-linkedin-evernote-hubspot-qa

12 LinkedIn Blog, Top 10 Overused LinkedIn Profile Buzzwords of 2013 blog.linkedin.com/2013/12/11/buzzwords-2013/

Chapter 10

13 2013 Jobvite Social Recruiting Survey Results, web.jobvite.com/rs/jobvite/images/Jobvite_SocialRecruiting2013.pdf

Chapter 13

14 Jennifer Grasz, *CareerBuilder Study Reveals Surprising Factors That Play a Part in Determining Who Gets Hired*, (CareerBuilder.com, August 28, 2013), http://www.careerbuilder.com/share/aboutus/pressreleasesdetail.aspx?sd=8%2F28%2F2013&id=pr778&ed=12%2F31%2F2013

Appendix A
LinkedIn Checklist

Settings

E-Mail Address—Have more than one e-mail address associated with your profile.	
Privacy Controls—Make sure to review the tabs labeled "Turn On/Off Your Activity Broadcasts" and "Select What Others See When You've Viewed Their Profile." Set up both of these to whatever matches your preference.	

Build Your Profile

Photo—You need a photo of yourself that is current and professional in nature. Your profile will be seven times more likely to be viewed if you include a photo.	
Headline—Use your branding statement. Think of this as your marketing tool. Don't just say, "I'm looking for a job."	
Summary—Tell others about yourself. What are you good at? What do you want to do? Try to distinguish yourself from others. Tell your story through the lens of the buyer.	
LinkedIn URL—Create a unique URL using your name. Add this link to your résumé.	
Public Profile—Search engines index your profile, and LinkedIn profiles receive a fairly high page rank in Google. At the least, make public your summary, current position, and education.	

Websites—You can list up to three URLs. When setting these up, always choose "Other," as this will allow you to customize the link. I recommend including a call to action.	
Twitter—If you have a Twitter handle, add it to your LinkedIn profile.	
Experience—Add your experience, but do not include every bullet point from your résumé. Highlight just your key successes, and do not list past positions that are not relevant to your current job search.	
Education—Include the degrees you have earned and any other academic awards you have received.	
Additional Sections—Add causes you support, volunteer service, honors, and awards (there are other sections you can add as well).	
Skills and Endorsements—List at least five skills (these will also be your keywords).	
Media Links—Include links to images, presentations, videos, and documents.	
Keywords—Use these many times in your profile.	
Recommendations—Give recommendations to others so they will reciprocate and give recommendations to you.	

Connect

Find people with whom you used to work, classmates, people who you served with, vendors, and clients via the "Advanced Search" tab.	
Import contacts from your online address book(s)—Gmail, AOL, Hotmail, Yahoo, and/or Outlook—via the "Add Connections" tab.	
Personalize the message when you send out the connection request. Use the opportunity to tell that person what you have been doing.	
Use LinkedIn contacts by saving notes on your connections' profiles and reaching out on birthdays, jobs changes, and anniversaries.	

Companies

Follow companies that interest you. Check out their "Jobs" tab.	
Do research on the company before your interview.	

Jobs

Set up multiple job alerts containing different keywords, and have them delivered to your e-mail account each day.	

Engage

Groups

Join groups company, school alumni, personal interests, location, and professional interests.	
Participate in group discussions at least twice a week.	
Connect with people who are in the same group.	
Check out the "Jobs" tab of the companies you're interested in.	

Be Active Daily!

Share status updates, remembering to keep it professional and brief. Attach a website link if there is one.	
Comment on or "like" others' updates.	

Mobile

Get LinkedIn app to help you stay in touch while you are on the go.	
Do research using your phone on the people who are interviewing you if you forget to do so before the interview.	
LinkedIn Job Search app- Standalone app to help find and apply for jobs	

Appendix B
Looking-for-Work Checklist

Connect with staffing agencies	
Contact references and put together a list with names, phone numbers, and e-mails	
Create or update your LinkedIn profile	
Develop "your brand"	
Develop five success/power stories	
Follow/Like companies on social media	
Have a professional e-mail address	
Have business cards	
Identify and build your network (who do you know?)	
Identify your support team	
Join networking groups	
List target companies you want to pursue	

Post your résumé to job websites (see Appendix C)	
Prepare your elevator speech/branding statement (this should be thirty seconds in length)	
Put together a general cover letter template	
Register for free weekly updates on TheLadders.com	
Set up alerts on Google, Indeed, Simply Hired, and LinkedIn	
Settings updated on Facebook	
Subscribe to a business journal and register for free daily updates	
Update your résumé and ask two people to review it	
Write down your values	

Weekly Goals

Add to your network (at least five new contacts)	
Contact people in your network (every day)	
Do in-person networking—attend a job-seeker group (at least once a week)	
Do in-person networking—pursue other contacts who are not job-seeker related (at least once a week)	
Follow up with target companies (at least two)	
Get out of the house (every day)	
Make time for yourself (every day)	
Post status updates on LinkedIn (every day)	
Set up informational interviews (at least one a week)	

Write down your goals for the week (do this over the weekend to be prepared for the workweek)	
Contact your network and provide a bi-monthly or quarterly update	
Update your résumé on job boards	
Volunteer in your community	

Monthly/Quarterly Goals

Contact your network and provide a bi-monthly or quarterly update	
Update your résumé on job boards	
Volunteer in your community	

Appendix C
Job and Networking Resources

Website	Description	App (iPhone and android)
www.abilityjobs.org	Employment of people with disabilities	android
jobs.aol.com	job alerts, employment info, career advice	
www.bullhornreach. com/jobs	Find jobs and recruiters	
www.careerbuilder. com	Job Postings and articles	iPhone and android
www.careeronestop.org	Find workforce services in your neighborhood or across the country	
www.craigslist.com	Provides job listings and forums to post résumé	iPhone and android

Website	Description	App (iPhone and android)
www.dice.com	Career site for technology and engineering professionals	iPhone and android
www.edjoin.com	Teaching and other education job openings	iPhone and android
www.flexjobs.com	Telecommuting, part-time, freelance, or flextime jobs	iPhone
www.glassdoor.com	Search through a huge database of company reviews, office photos, CEO approval ratings	iPhone and android
www.hoovers.com	Researching companies and industries	
www.idealist.org	Jobs abroad, nonprofit careers, volunteer opportunities	
www.indeed.com	Metasearch engine site that aggregates job listings from thousands of websites, including job boards, newspapers, associations, and company career pages	iPhone and android

Website	Description	App (iPhone and android)
www.ldsjobs.org	LDS Employment Resource Services	
www.theladders.com	Site for career professionals, job postings, great articles, job matching	iPhone and android
www.manta.com	Research businesses	
Website	**Description**	**App (iPhone and android)**
www.monster.com	Job postings and articles	iPhone and android
www.simplyhired.com	Metasearch engine site that aggregates job listings from thousands of websites, including job boards, newspapers, associations, and company career pages	iPhone and android
www.tweetmyjobs.com	Social and mobile recruitment and job distribution network matching job seekers with employers	iPhone and android
www.usajobs.gov	Federal Government's official source for federal job listings	iPhone and android
www.vault.com	Get inside scoop on companies	

Check other websites: city, county, state, local chamber, college and/or university career center, alumni groups, professional organizations		
Networking Websites		
www.meetup.com	Find networking groups in your area	iPhone and android
Website	**Description**	**App (iPhone and android)**
www.toastmasters.com	Communication and leadership development	
Resources		
www.ActiveJobSeekers. org	Providing support, networking, and employment opportunities to individuals online and offline	
www.careerbliss.com	Company reviews and ratings, salary info and jobs.	
www.careerealism.com	Job Resource. Sign up to get daily career tips.	
www.cns.gov	More information on volunteer opportunities	
www.evernote.com	Scan business cards	iPhone and android

Website	Description	App (iPhone and android)
www. futureproofyourcareer. com	Career testing	
www.gcflearnfree. org/facebook101/1	Free program to learn more about Facebook	iPhone and android
www.slideshare.net	Sharing and viewing PowerPoint presentations	
Website	**Description**	**App (iPhone and android)**
www.mbopartners.com	Helping Independent Contractors	
www.keirsey.com	Career testing	iPhone
www.neighbors-helping-neighbors.com	East Coast organization-targeted to adults who are actively looking for work and interested in reinvigorating their careers and undertaking a job search campaign.	
www.salary.com	Research compensation	iPhone
www.sba.gov	Resources for starting a business	iPhone and android
www.score.org	Local representatives give free small business advice	
www.theblogstarter. com	Step-by-step instructor of how to start your own blog.	

www.vistaprint.com	Supplier to print business cards	iPhone
www.visualcv.com	Highlight professional accomplishments in a personal visualization	
www.vizualize.me	Highlight professional accomplishments in a personal visualization	iPhone
Website	**Description**	**App (iPhone and android)**
www.whatsforwork.com	Helping women take control of their careers. Job postings, great webinars and articles	
www.wordle.net	Program for generating word clouds from text that you provide	iPhone
Media Websites		
www.bizjournals.com	Research companies and what is going to on in a specific metro area	iPhone
www.google.com/alerts	Set up alerts	iPhone and android
Recommended Books		
Now, Discover Your Strengths	by Marcus Buckingham	

Find Your Strongest Life: What the Happiest and Most Successful Women Do Differently	by Marcus Buckingham	
What Color is your Parachute	by Richard N Bolles	
Identity: Passport to Freedom	By Stedman Graham	
Social Media Sites		
www.linkedin.com	#1 online professional network	iPhone and android
www.twitter.com	Real time source of information	iPhone and android
Website	**Description**	**App (iPhone and android)**
www.pinterest.com	Collect ideas for projects and different interests	iPhone and android
www.facebook.com	Online social networking	iPhone and android
www.youtube.com	Video sharing website	iPhone and android
www.plus.google.com	Discovering and sharing digital content	iPhone and android

Appendix D
Veteran Resources

Website	Description	App (iPhone and android)
www. calvet.ca.gov	California Veterans- Education, Employment, Healthcare, Housing, Advocacy, VA Claims	iPhone and android
www. careers4life.org	NEAT- National Education, Advocacy and Training- Helping Veterans find employment	
www. farmvetco.org	Careers in Agriculture	
www. h2h.jobs	Hero to Hired- Job postings, hiring events	iPhone, android
www. msepjobs. militaryonesource.mil	Military Spouse Employment Partnership	
www. mst.vaforvets. va.gov/mst/va/ mos-translator	Feds for Vets MOS translator, job search, career assessments	

Website	Description	App (iPhone and android)
www. nrd.g	National Resource Directory connecting service members, veterans, their families with resources.	
www. vaforvets.va.gov	Veterans and transitioning military find federal and non-profit careers	
www. veterans. linkedin.com	Veteran Mentor Network group. Information on 1 year free job seeker subscription	
www. vets.syr.edu	Institute Veterans Military Families	
www. vets101.org	Free career planning tools	
www.benefits.va.gov/ vocrehab/index.asp	Vocational Rehabilitation and Employment	
www.dol.gov/vets/	Veteran's Employment and Training Services	
www.dvba.org	California Disabled Veteran Business Alliance	
www.esgr.mil	Employer Support of the Guard and Reserve	
www.fedshirevets.gov/ job/veterans.aspx	Job Resource	
Website	Description	App (iPhone and android)
www.hireahero.org	Job Postings, Salary research	

Website	Description	App (iPhone and android)
www.hireheroes.org	Employment assistance and job boards	
www.military.com/ veteran-jobs	Military Friendly jobs, Military skills translator, Career Expo	iPhone
www. militaryonesource. mil/transition	Military OneSource Transition Assistance Resources	
www.moaa.org/career	Military Officers Association of America Resources	
www.navoba.com	National Veteran Owned Business Association	
www. onetonline. org	O*NET OnLine- database containing occupation specific descriptors.	
www.rallypoint.com	US Military Professional Network	
www.swords-to-plowshares.org	Provides employment and training to Vets in SF Bay Area	
www. taonline.com/ APOffice	Careers for Transitioning military. Transition Assistance Program	
Website	**Description**	**App (iPhone and android)**
www.vamboa.org	Veteran and Military Business Owners Association	

Appendix E
Master Application

Employment Application

Full Name: _____ Date:_____
　　　　　　　Last　　　　　　　　　First　　　　　　　　　M.I.

Address: _____
　　　　　Street Address　　　　　　　　　　　　　　　　Apartment/Unit #

　　　　　_____
　　　　　City　　　　　　　　　　　　　　　　State　　　ZIP Code

Phone: _____ Email _____

Date Available: _____ Social Security No.:_____ Desired Salary:$_____

Position Applied for: _____

　　　　　　　　　　　　　　　　　　　YES　NO
Are you a citizen of the United States? ☐　☐　If no, are you authorized to work in the U.S.? YES ☐　NO ☐

　　　　　　　　　　　　　　　　　　　YES　NO
Have you ever worked for this company? ☐　☐　If yes, when?_____

　　　　　　　　　　　　　　　　　　　YES　NO
Have you ever been convicted of a felony? ☐　☐

If yes, explain: _____

Education

High School: _____ Address:_____

From: _____ To:_____ Did you graduate? YES ☐ NO ☐ Diploma::_____

College: _____ Address:_____

From: _____ To:_____ Did you graduate? YES ☐ NO ☐ Degree:_____

Other: _____ Address:_____

From: _____ To:_____ Did you graduate? YES ☐ NO ☐ Degree:_____

References

Please list three professional references.

Full Name: _____ Relationship:_____

Company: _____ Phone:_____

Address: _____

125

Full Name: _____   Relationship: _____
Company: _____   Phone: _____
Address: _____

Full Name: _____   Relationship: _____
Company: _____   Phone: _____
Address: _____

Previous Employment

Company: _____   Phone: _____
Address: _____   Supervisor: _____

Job Title: _____   Starting Salary:$ _____   Ending Salary:$ _____

Responsibilities: _____

From: _____   To: _____   Reason for Leaving: _____

May we contact your previous supervisor for a reference?   YES ☐   NO ☐

Company: _____   Phone: _____
Address: _____   Supervisor: _____

Job Title: _____   Starting Salary:$ _____   Ending Salary:$ _____

Responsibilities: _____

From: _____   To: _____   Reason for Leaving: _____

May we contact your previous supervisor for a reference?   YES ☐   NO ☐

Company: _____   Phone: _____
Address: _____   Supervisor: _____

Job Title: _____   Starting Salary:$ _____   Ending Salary:$ _____

Responsibilities: _____

From: _____   To: _____   Reason for Leaving: _____

May we contact your previous supervisor for a reference?   YES ☐   NO ☐

Military Service

Branch: _____ From: _____ To: _____

Rank at Discharge: _____ Type of Discharge: _____

If other than honorable, explain: _____

Disclaimer and Signature

I certify that my answers are true and complete to the best of my knowledge.

If this application leads to employment, I understand that false or misleading information in my application or interview may result in my release.

Signature: _____ Date: _____

Lightning Source UK Ltd.
Milton Keynes UK
UKOW04f1138110515

251261UK00002B/552/P